Traditional Domestic
Architecture of Japan

Volume 21
THE HEIBONSHA SURVEY OF JAPANESE ART

For a list of the entire series see end of book

CONSULTING EDITORS

Katsuichiro Kamei, *art critic*
Seiichiro Takahashi, *Chairman, Japan Art Academy*
Ichimatsu Tanaka, *Chairman, Cultural Properties Protection Commission*

Traditional Domestic Architecture of Japan

by TEIJI ITOH

translated by Richard L. Gage

New York · WEATHERHILL/HEIBONSHA · Tokyo

This book was originally published in Japanese by Heibonsha under the title *Minka* in the Nihon no Bijutsu Series.

First English Edition, 1972
Third Printing, 1979

Jointly published by John Weatherhill, Inc., of New York and Tokyo, with editorial offices at 7-6-13 Roppongi, Minato-ku, Tokyo 106, Japan, and Heibonsha, Tokyo. Copyright © 1965, 1972, by Heibonsha; all rights reserved. Printed in Japan.

LCC Card No. 76-183520   ISBN 0-8348-1004-2

Contents

1. The Traditional House in the World of Today   9

2. The Minka Design Method   42

    Floor Plans and Post Placement   42

    Basic Structures   43

    The Post as Symbol   51

    Functional Durability   53

    The Area Under the Eaves   55

3. The Development of Special Minka Characteristics   70

    Regional Traits and Social Symbolism   70

    Roof-Truss Structures   72

    The Influence of Roof Structures on Floor Plans   109

    Module Based on Tatami or Interpost Span   112

    Marking Structural Members   115

    Regional Status Symbols   118

    The Strength and Weakness of Sumptuary Edicts   125

4. Before the Minka   127

5. The Minka from Medieval to Early Modern Times   134

    Houses of the Heian and Kamakura Periods   134

    The Rin'ami House and the Jitogata Mandokoro   138

    Sennenya   139

    Urban Houses of Sixteenth-Century Nara and
Kyoto   140

Houses of the Early Edo Period   143

6.   Shops and Farmhouses of the Edo Period   145

Shops of the Edo Period   145

Farmhouses of the Edo Period   148

Traditional Domestic
Architecture of Japan

The Traditional House in the World of Today

THE VERANDA on which I sit is old and ramshackle. Over me hangs a rush-thatched roof that seems to be a meter thick. From under the eaves all I can see is the lower reaches of a mountain in the distance. The hot sun of early summer is making that mountain blindingly bright and painful to look at. All I can hear is the murmuring of a mountain river to the east of the house and the chirping of the cicadas. But no, even though they are called pine cicadas, they really aren't cicadas at all, I am told.

It has not been very long since the eaves, supported by thick bark-covered posts, hung even lower, and not even the foothills of the distant mountain, let alone the sky, were visible from where I sit. At that time nothing but another part of the house and the nearby fields could be seen. In the more remote past a combination gate and gatehouse, quarters for retainers of the owner of the house, blocked even the fields from view.

Long ago, after bending to pass under the eaves and into the house, one found himself in a spacious plank-floored room in the center of which was a sunken hearth. In summer as well as in winter a charcoal fire glowed there, and water was always on the boil in an iron kettle. Even at midday this room was dark, and dark it remains today. But there is no longer a hearth, and the old plank flooring has been covered with ten *tatami* mats. Among the mats, however, there are gaps about fifteen centimeters wide that have been filled with long boards. It may well be that *tatami* were used in this house from the very beginning, but the gaps suggest that it was built before it became the custom to cover the entire floor of a room with them. Indeed, this house has stood for some five to six centuries, and the gaps among the *tatami* bear witness to the changing ages it has seen.

Now, several times a day, buses come rumbling into the remote village in the mountain valley where this house stands. The much-pitted and rutted road is only four meters wide, and two buses cannot pass each other unless one of them retreats well to the side. Passengers alight in front of a small shrine, and the next stop on the route is the end of the line. Even this narrow road was not built until the middle of the nineteenth century. In the age when the land was divided into great manors, officials probably traveled this same road, but at that time it was only a raised pathway among the rice paddies. In the sixteenth century the armed warriors of the military dictator Toyotomi Hideyoshi, bent on the conquest of Korea and China, may have raged along that same path with the violence of a storm.

When the disastrous ten-year Onin War broke out in Kyoto in 1467, a certain samurai, though by

1. *Detail of roof of Hakogi* sennenya *(thousand-year house), probably fourteenth or fifteenth century, Yamada-cho, Hyogo-ku, Kobe. (See also Figures 12, 151.)*

no means a warrior of great fame or wealth, controlled this village and lived in this house. Having been called into service, he provided his few soldiers with food and bows and arrows and set out with them for the capital. But the fortunes of war were against him, and he soon lost his life in battle. His widow, left behind to mourn him, may well have watched the pale sun momentarily pierce the clouds from which passing showers of rain fell on the village and for an instant illumine the colored leaves of the mountainside trees, for it was late autumn when the samurai went to his death.

But what was the state of her dwelling when tragedy struck this lady? It then consisted of only two rooms. One of these, about the size of six *tatami* mats (about ten square meters), was a combination sleeping quarters and storage space for what treasured articles the family possessed. Their beds were simple pallets of rice straw, for cotton wadding was not introduced into Japan until about the Temmon era (1532–55), and, though silk floss was available to people of means, it would have been

far beyond the humble aspirations of a family of this status. Aside from the board door that hung on sunken pivots at its entrance, this room had no other openings.

The other room was the scene of most daily activities, including meals and the entertainment of guests. Although the wall between it and the storage-sleeping room was only adze-finished, its surface was beautifully polished, and on it hung a scroll painting of either the gentle Buddha Amida or the ferocious-looking but benevolent Buddhist deity Aizen Myo-o. Such paintings were indications of the devout religious attitude of the master of the house. In addition to these two genuine rooms there was an earth-floored area of about sixteen square meters where the cooking was done and the lowlier members of the household slept.

Cramped indeed to modern eyes, this house, at the time it was built, was a fine dwelling: the kind of home thought suitable to a rural samurai. The successive masters of the household lived as cultivators of the land in times of peace. Sometimes they

2. *Home of Uruma Tokikuni, father of Honen Shonin, as pictured in the fourteenth-century picture scroll* Honen Shonin Eden *(Pictorial Life of Saint Honen)*, Chion-in, Kyoto.

were called to do guard duty in the capital city of Kyoto or to perform other duties at the castle of the lord of the local fief. But even when they were encamped for some truly military purpose, these men are known to have returned to the village for the important Rokujo Hachiman Festival in the autumn.

Finally, in 1580, the day came when the family had to abandon military life entirely. After the forces to which they were partisan met resounding defeat at the hands of the powerful military dictator and ruler of the land Toyotomi Hideyoshi, they became farmers exclusively. For this turn of events we may be grateful, for, had luck been with the family to the extent that they became lords of a castle of their own, or had they clung to the samurai calling and abandoned their home for some castle town, this marvelous old house, known to us today as the Hakogi *sennenya*, or thousand-year house of the Hakogi family (Figs. 1, 12, 151), would have been destroyed forever.

About one hundred years later, when this area had become an agricultural district under the direct control of the Tokugawa shogunate, a certain official named Kobori Jin'emon, on making an inspection tour, came upon this house and gave it the appellation *sennenya*. This took place in the seventeenth century. Today, should any of our contemporaries discover a house dating from that century, it would naturally be considered a remarkable antique, but even as early as the seventeenth century this house was thought to be an ancient rarity. At present only a few posts from the original structure remain, and these are decayed, split vertically, scarred, and marked with tenons and mortises, some of which are of a very old and now unusual type. Virtually none of the posts seem to have the strength to support the beams resting on them, and certainly not a single one appears capable of bearing the heavy roof. To a casual observer, the old house must look wretched indeed. In fact, many people are concerned that a typhoon or an earthquake might tumble it to the ground. Still, in all likelihood, the house has been in much the same

3. *Outbuildings of Hikobe house, seventeenth century, Kiryu, Gumma Prefecture.*

shape for two hundred years and perhaps longer. Why has no one torn it down? Why have its inhabitants tolerated patent inconvenience over the generations when technological and cultural advances were being made for the improvement of comfort in human living? It may well be that the reason lies in a conviction that the so-called conveniences of modern society, which threaten our very future existence instead of elevating human happiness, do not and cannot maintain this house and what it stands for. Perhaps the occupants have believed that the age of a building is a more trustworthy status symbol than any human invention.

THE HAKOGI *sennenya* is a house of the type known as the *minka*: literally, "people's house" or perhaps "folk house" but more specifically "commoner's house" and distinguished from the more pretentious residences of the ruling class in the feudal period. Since there is really no satisfactory English equivalent for the term, it will be most convenient to use the Japanese word *minka* from this point on.

My readers may wonder why I have spent so

much time discussing this old house. It is because I love it as much as its owner does. History, no matter how well organized and systematized theoretically, has little effect on one's basic philosophy of life as long as it remains no more than a cerebral and "fictional" composition. It becomes easier to assimilate when it is understood through the senses, as it is in the case of these old houses, which one can actually see. Excellent historical writings are like novels because they are understandable to people of all personalities. The *minka*, however, is more vivid because it exists before our eyes in its natural and historical state. Since I consider its dramatic presence in its ancient environment the most important aspect of the *minka*, I naturally regard placing such venerable houses in museums or in reconstructed "*minka* villages," as they are called, in very much the same way I regard old folks' homes—that is, inevitable. If left in their natural settings, in too many cases the old houses would vanish completely. Therefore we take them away and reconstruct them in some area where they are safe but where they at the same time become mummies with no hope of resuscitation. Today, of

4. *Gate to Egawa house, formerly a village mayor's residence, eighteenth century, Nirayama, Shizuoka Prefecture. (See also Figure 145.)*

course, although many people build houses in the *minka* style or incorporate *minka* elements in shops and residences, no one builds a *minka* in the true and ancient sense. Farmers find it difficult to obtain the miscanthus reeds traditionally used in thatching. Moreover, they find maintaining thatched roofs a burdensome and irksome task. Families complain that the *minka* is inconvenient, that it affords no privacy. Some go so far as to refuse flatly to continue living in the *minka* they own. Houses that are being built today to be torn down tomorrow are residences, to be sure, but no one can call them *minka*.

Is it possible, then, to say that the *minka* is losing its social significance? No one doubts that when a thing is devoid of importance to society it loses its reason for existence and therefore must vanish, as did the primeval Japanese pit dwellings. In order to preserve the *minka* in some form or other, we must move them to outdoor museums—collections of ghost houses—where they are kept as ornaments and relics of the past. I am convinced that the *minka* is at its most attractive and beautiful only when it is restored to the condition of its initial

construction, even if in that condition it is difficult to live in and inconvenient from a modern point of view. In other words, attempts to conform the *minka* to the needs of modern living inevitably detract from the beauty of the house. Without doubt this is one of the great tragedies of this architectural genre, born and developed in a feudal society yet lingering on in an entirely different social world. If this is true, has the time come for us to abandon the *minka* completely? If, as we look toward the life of the future, our appreciation of the beauty of the *minka* requires excessive concern with conservative attitudes and restorations, it may already be too late to save it. Nostalgia alone cannot revive the social significance of the *minka*. Nevertheless, the *minka* does offer suggestions for the architectural ideology of today. I believe that Japanese architects, when they feel that the architectural ideas of our time have bogged down, turn their gaze toward the *minka* because it seems to reveal directly a certain innate spatial concept that is at once meaningful and symbolic. Still, when people discard things or ignore them, the reason usually is that they can no longer find any present value in

6. Onigawara (ornamental roof tile), Takakura house, Hiji, Oita Prefecture.

5. Gable detail of Imanishi house, seventeenth century (1650), Imai-cho, Kashihara, Nara Prefecture. (See also Figures 40, 46, 67, 74.)

them. In this respect it may be that the vanishing *minka* must leave only an empty shell of its former self.

UP TO NOW, books about the *minka* have discussed it in terms of its historical development, its ethnic characteristics, and its regional distribution—all significant aspects of the *minka*, to be sure. Fortunately there are already many fine books that deal with it from these points of view. For this reason, there is no need for me to comment at length about such matters, and I should like, instead, to deal with the *minka* in terms of its spatial design. Of course, spatial design is one of the most fundamental aspects of the study of architecture, but attempting to discuss it as it exists in the *minka* is to a certain extent adventurous, since research on the subject has so far produced insufficient results. My own study will owe much to the work of others in the field.

I have long felt—and I felt it even more intensely when I was teaching Western students about spatial concepts in architecture—that the *minka* contains a condensation of suggestions for modern architectural ideology. Telling the story of the *minka* involves dissecting its spatial personality and discovering its meaning for today, but at the same time the tale itself is certainly a reflection of contemporary architectural movements and of the philosophies and ideologies that we, as instigators of those movements, are bound to hold. But before analyzing the spatial concepts of the *minka* I must define more precisely the nature of the architectural genre.

In ethnological parlance a *minka* is a residence of the folk, the people who live permanently in a given locality, but architecturally what kind of residence is it? No one can contest the inclusion in this category of both the farmhouses and the urban

7. *Takemura house, seventeenth century (1684), Komagane, Nagano Prefecture.*

houses built in Japan during the feudal period. A retrospective of the lineage of the *minka*, however, shows that the Japanese have produced two other traditional residential styles completely different from the *minka*: the *shinden* and the *shoin* homes of the aristocratic and the wealthy. Since the floor plans of the two differ sharply from that of the *minka*, they have been justly afforded separate treatment in architectural history. The separation between these two styles—on the one hand the non-*minka*, if I may so call them, and on the other the true *minka*—reflects the difference between the rulers, who dwelt in the *shinden* and *shoin* homes, and the ruled, who lived in the *minka*. And it is immediately obvious that architectural differences between the *minka* and the non-*minka* extend to elevation, external appearance, and structural details.

There is one type of feudal-period house, however, that does not conveniently fit into either of these two classifications. This is the residence of the typical samurai. Examples of houses embodying elements of both the *minka* and the non-*minka* styles can be found as early as the Kamakura (1185–1336) and the Muromachi (1336–1568) periods. There can be little doubt that the residence of Minamoto Yoritomo, founder of the Kamakura shogunate, was very much like the *shinden* mansions of Kyoto noblemen in the Heian period (794–1185). The thirteenth-century picture scroll *Moko Shurai Ekotoba*, dealing with the attempted Mongol invasions of Japan in 1274 and 1281, makes it clear that a certain Akita Shironosuke, a warrior-retainer of the shogun, lived in a house closely resembling the mansions of the Kyoto aristocrats. If retainers enjoyed such splendor, it seems unlikely that the leader of the nation, the shogun Yoritomo himself, would have lived on a scale less grand. The mansions of the Ashikaga shoguns, who ruled the nation

8. Irori *(sunken hearth)*, *Kita house, nineteenth century, Nonoichi, Ishikawa Prefecture. (See also Figures 36, 42.)*

9 *(bottom left). Lantern at Echigoya inn, nineteenth century, Naraijuku, Narakawa, Nagano Prefecture.*

10 *(bottom right). Entrance to interior storehouse of Omiya shop, nineteenth century, Yamagata City, Yamagata Prefecture. (See also Figure 95.)*

11. Shirakawa farmhouse in gassho style, eighteenth century, Shirakawa Village, Gifu Prefecture.

12. *Hakogi* sennenya *(thousand-year house), probably fourteenth or fifteenth century, Yamada-cho, Hyogo-ku, Kobe. (See also Figures 1, 151.)*

13. *Urban houses in Gojozaka, Higashiyama, Kyoto, with Kiyomizu Temple in the background.*

14. *Restored* minka *from Akiyama, Nagano Prefecture, eighteenth century, now in* minka *village, Toyonaka, Osaka Prefecture.*

during the Muromachi period, were as pretentious as any in the land, although, of course, they varied according to the time when they were built and showed the transition from the *shinden* to the *shoin* style. We find proof of this in the portrayal of the shogun's mansion on a sixteenth-century painted screen depicting sights in and around Kyoto. We also learn from this same source that the residence of the shogun's deputy was of the same style as that of the shogun. In fact, a number of screens from this time show the houses of high-ranking samurai who patently preferred to model their dwellings on the tastes of the ancient capital.

Nevertheless, during the Muromachi period, certain samurai homes were indistinguishable in style from ordinary farmhouses of the *minka* type. We have already noted a classical example of such samurai residences in the Hakogi *sennenya*, which is one of a number of such "thousand-year houses"

once found in Hyogo Prefecture. Although these houses were *minka* in the fullest sense of the word, they were the homes of rural samurai. They and other similar samurai dwellings are the prototypes of the *minka* in Hyogo Prefecture, as one can easily see from a comparison of their structures and plans with those of later houses in the region. The samurai who lived in the *sennenya* were also part-time farmers—that is, their way of life was one that was to become common in certain parts of Japan after the establishment of the Tokugawa shogunate and the resultant pacification of the country in the early seventeenth century.

What I have been saying clearly points to a sharp distinction between the *minka* and the non-*minka* and suggests that the line of distinction correlates with social strata in Japanese feudal society. There are, however, some interestingly misleading cases. For example, in the fourteenth-century picture

15. *Front view of Yoshimura house, seventeenth century, Habikino, Osaka Prefecture. (See also Figures 22, 39, 48, 93, 107, 123.)*

scroll *Honen Shonin Eden,* which is an illustrated life of the great Kamakura priest Honen Shonin, we see a picture of the home of Honen Shonin's father, who was an *oryoshi*—that is, a police commissioner or high sheriff. The house (Fig. 2) is supposed to have stood in the province of Mimasaka (modern Okayama Prefecture) around 1140. From the standpoint of building materials, it is very like a *minka,* for it has a thatched main roof with a surrounding plank skirting roof. Certain other features smack strongly of the influence of the lower-ranking aristocratic mansions of the big city. The presence of eaves running around the main section, the *shitomido* (lattice doors that swing upward to be held in place by rods suspended from the ceiling), the absence of an earth-floored room, the corridor wing leading from the gate to the main part of the house, and the separate kitchen building are all aspects foreign to the *minka* and common to most noblemen's homes of the period. Another picture in the same scroll shows a house in which Honen Shonin stopped for a night on his way into exile. It too is most certainly a variation of the Kyoto *shinden*-style mansion. It is perfectly possible that the artistic versions of these houses sprang from nothing but the imagination of the artist, but it is generally accepted as a fact that the home of Honen Shonin's father and that of his host for a night on his unhappy journey into banishment were simplifications of the *shinden* style. Moreover, houses of this class were described in official records by means of terminology that cannot be, or at any rate never was, used to describe *minka.* The difference in terminology is possibly connected in some way with tax assessment.

I have said something about the houses of the Kamakura and Muromachi periods and a little about the stylistic differences between the houses of the rulers and the ruled after the establishment of the Tokugawa shogunate in 1603, but when we

16. *Izumo-style* minka, *eighteenth century, Hirata, Shimane Prefecture.*

turn our attention to the so-called Sengoku, or Warring Provinces, period (1482–1558), which intervened between earlier and later ages of greater political stability, we find some more interesting things about the houses in which people lived. Let me take as an example the military dictator Toyotomi Hideyoshi, who laid the groundwork of unification on which the success of the Tokugawa shogunate was founded. Some hold that Hideyoshi was the son of a poor farmer; others claim that he came from the family of a foot soldier. For the sake of this discussion it makes no difference which version is true, for in either case the home of his youth would have been of the *minka* category. At the time of his death, however, he was residing in a glittering mansion in the compound of Osaka Castle. Nothing could have been further from a *minka* than the scene of his demise. The mansion at Osaka Castle was certainly of the *shoin* style, as were the other great residences that Hideyoshi built, including the Jurakudai, Fushimi, and Yodo castle-palaces.

In short, until a certain time in his life, Hideyoshi lived in buildings belonging to the *minka* tradition, and after that time he lived in homes of the category that had developed as the residences of the ruling class. In other words, at some time during his lifetime that style of the building in which he maintained permanent domicile completely altered. Furthermore, it is not so much that, as he slowly rose through the levels of society, he gradually improved the quality of his home as that at a single point in time he came to live in buildings entirely different from those in which he had lived until then. Since information on the house in which he was born and on his earlier homes is wanting, it is impossible to say for certain just when this change occurred, but common sense leads one to select the year 1583, when Osaka Castle was being built, or some time a bit earlier.

Be all of this as it may, it is clear that the Japa-

17. *Tsubokawa house, seventeenth century, Maruoka, Fukui Prefecture.*

19 *(opposite page, left).* Oni- ▷
gawara (ornamental roof tile), Naka house, seventeenth century, Kumatori, Osaka Prefecture. (See also Figures 73, 87.)

20 *(opposite page, right).* Shoji ▷
door, Horiuchi house, eighteenth century, Shiojiri, Nagano Prefecture. (See also Figures 100, 108, 121.)

18. *Front view of Arikabe* honjin, *formerly an inn for daimyo, eighteenth century, Arikabe, Kannari, Miyagi Prefecture.*

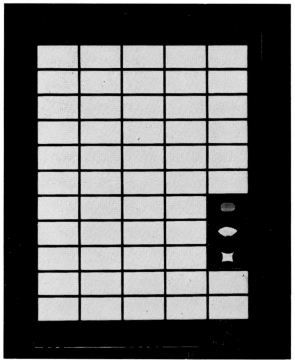

nese house followed two radically different lines of development, both of which find direct reflection in the plans, sections, external appearances, and structures of the buildings themselves. Moreover, Japanese culture could not very well do without either tradition. Although many people have been born and raised in *minka* and have gained experience of them through direct contact, the history of the systematic architectural study of the houses is very short. Research on the *minka* from the ethnic viewpoint has been in progress for more than fifty years, but, with the exception of a few forward-looking people, no one undertook their architectural study until about ten years ago. The very appellation *minka,* though it appears in Chinese works as old of those of the Former Han period (206 B.C. to A.D. 8), offers some problems, especially when attempts are made to translate it into other languages.

Sometimes the word *minka* is rendered as "rural house," but this is inaccurate because certain kinds of urban dwellings also fall into the *minka* category. "People's house" has a meaning far wider than the Japanese term implies, and "public house" incurs the danger of confusion with "tavern," although it is true that the *minka* genre includes certain types of post-town inns of the feudal period (Figs. 18, 34, 65, 97, 98). When all is said and done, there seems to be no accurate translation for the term, and for that reason, as I have noted earlier, I have decided that *minka* is the only proper word to use.

HISTORY IS something written in the present by people whose historical view is that of the present. Stated poetically, so to speak, this means that the present time recreates history that has already passed. It is for the very reason that the present has its own ideology that a history suitable to another age can be established. The history of the *minka* is no exception to this general rule. The *minka* has

long been a mirror in which it is possible to read the architectural ideologies of other ages. In some periods, the *minka* itself was not there to serve this function, whereas in others it reflected the sorrows and stagnation of the architecture of the times as well as new architectural ideologies then being evolved for the sake of a coming era. The *minka* always faces the past, but architectural ideology is always turned toward the future. When these two lines of vision intersect, at their junction they always reveal some new aspect of the *minka* and thus further its development. Historically speaking, these intersections have occurred in three instances.

The tea masters of the sixteenth century, finding an aesthetic prototype in the *minka*, were the first people ever to regard these houses as objects of beauty. By discovering a mellow loveliness in the *minka* and elevating that beauty to the level of art, these men gave birth to the teahouse style of architecture and the *sukiya* residential style that grew out

of it. In addition, through the medium of the teahouse, these men liberated architectural design from the religious bonds imposed on it in earlier centuries. During the years preceding the sixteenth century both gardening and architecture employed imagery taken from Buddhist philosophy, but the teahouse was thought of as nothing more than a purely beautiful place in which to perform the tea ceremony. The *minka* was the mediating prototype in the visualization and formalization of this beautiful place. The contribution of the tea masters in discovering a completely different kind of value in the *minka* is especially apparent when one realizes that the feudal lords of the Kamakura and Muromachi periods regarded the *minka* as nothing but objects of taxation or domiciles of rural civil servants. The fact that most of the tea masters were men of the nonaristocratic, nonmilitary town culture is not unrelated to the nature of their achievement.

For some three and a half centuries following the

◁ *21. Sakamotojuku, formerly a post town on the Nakasendo highway, Sakamoto, Gumma Prefecture*

22. Beamwork and reed ceiling, Yoshimura house, seventeenth century, Habikino, Osaka Prefecture. (See also Figures 15, 39, 48, 93, 107, 123.)

Muromachi period the *minka* existed in more or less the forms in which it is known today, and throughout that long period no conscious effort, save that of the tea masters, was made to find new architectural values in it. Even worse, during the eighteenth and early nineteenth centuries the *minka* was largely ignored except as an objective of the prohibitive sumptuary edicts issued by the feudal government.

The Western architectural ideas and techniques that flooded the nation at the opening of the Meiji era (1868–1912) had no effect on the *minka* and failed to uncover any new aspects in the old residential style. In the 1920's, however, when the modern architectural movement reached Japan, the *minka* as part of the Japanese residential architectural tradition assumed certain new colorations in the minds of the people. First of all, within the *minka* was to be found a prototype of the qualities prized by modern architecture: simplicity, clarity,

lack of ornamentation, and distinctive structure and design. During his several trips to Japan, after having been banished from Germany by the Nazis, the architect Bruno Taut brought this interpretation of the values of the *minka* to maximum public attention.

A little later the *minka* was elevated as a model of the kind of functional planning dear to the hearts of modern architectural designers. Since the *fusuma* (sliding partitions) and *shoji* (sliding doors) of the *minka* may be removed at will, the spaces may be freely varied in size (Figs. 63, 96). The functional flexibility allowing varied uses of a single room was considered a symbol of both inseparably mixed public and private living functions and the poverty that forbade indulgence in large spaces. No matter that the *minka* was by no means designed in accordance with functionalism. Not only was it lauded as verification of the validity of the functionalists' theories; it was also said to be characterized by this

23. Nineteenth-century minka *in Hirosaki, Aomori Prefecture.*

very functional flexibility. This is an excellent example of the process by means of which we seek to find new things in the *minka*. First, by digging into its past we attempt to find suggestions for the present. Then, by analyzing the present we strive to develop an ideology for the future. Nevertheless, the fruits of functionalism are abundantly apparent today, and many architects are fully aware of the limits of this approach.

The present day is the third point in time at which some new aspect of the *minka* is being uncovered. Although functionalism is now ebbing, no ideology has yet arrived to take its place. Many people are making efforts to produce ideologies, but these appear and disappear without leaving anything of lasting value behind. It may be, of course, that within all the apparent futility there can be found an idea that future ages will accept. The prevailing conditions today are not unlike those that plagued Japanese architecture in the seventeenth century and again in the late nineteenth century.

The nature of the definitive new guiding ideology for architecture is not known, but I believe that a philosophy of symbolism is gradually assuming an increasingly important position in the reigning confusion. It is not necessarily true that this philosophy of symbolism, if codified and fed into a computer for the sake of developing an organizational and technological basis for environmental design, will then inevitably guide the architectural ideology of tomorrow. Nevertheless, design based on symbols is emerging, and it undeniably has the power to attract people.

At any rate, there are people today who attempt to evaluate the *minka* in the light of the philosophy of symbols. When I discussed a number of design systems with students at the University of Washing-

24. Minka *in Yamashita, Sonobe, Kyoto Prefecture.*

25. *Port town of Murotsu on the Seto Inland Sea, Hyogo Prefecture.*

26. Minka *in Takachiho, Miyazaki Prefecture.*

27. *Niijuku, formerly a post town on the Nanagajuku highway, Takabatake, Yamagata Prefecture.*

28. *Naraijuku, formerly a post town on the Kiso highway, Narakawa Village, Nagano Prefecture.*

29. Gassho-style farmhouses (Shira-kawa houses) in Kamitaira Village, Toyama Prefecture.

30. *Fishermen's houses surrounded by stone walls as protection against typhoons, Sotodomari, Nishiumi, Ehime Prefecture.*

31. *Farmhouses in Higashi Iyayama Village, Tokushima Prefecture.*

32. *Farmhouses of the Izumo district, Hikawa Village, Shimane Prefecture.*

33. Residential blocks in city of Omi Hachiman, Shiga Prefecture.

34. *Earth-floored area of Yagumo* honjin, *formerly an inn for daimyo, eighteenth century, Shinji, Shimane Prefecture. (See also Figures 65, 89, 97.)*

ton, many of them felt that the *minka* was the most suggestive. Of course, this does not imply the direct application to modern architecture of unaltered *minka* design. It is interesting, however, to observe that the principle of *minka* design is non-Western in that it does not result in one fixed external form but instead makes possible a wide variety of exterior appearances.

There are marked regional differences in all aspects of the *minka*, including plans, forms, and details. Not surprisingly, regional differences in roof form and ridge ornament—obvious to anyone —were the first thing to be commented on by ethnologists. These characteristics, as well as others, were probably essential in the feudal age when the *minka* was developed. Certainly regional differences are one of the most noteworthy traits of the *minka*, but before I discuss them I must point out the elements that *minka* throughout Japan have in common.

CHAPTER TWO

The Minka Design Method

FLOOR PLANS AND POST PLACEMENT Although the modern architect draws up a wide variety of plans for a building—floor plan, elevations, sections, perspectives, plans for beams and roof, and the like—the carpenter of the past, who was the man responsible for designing most traditional Japanese buildings, including the *minka,* satisfied all his needs with nothing more than a floor plan. In building teahouses, it is true, carpenters sometimes employed a kind of perspective drawing called an *oshiezu,* but this was always used in dealing with copies of tearoom types, and it by no means represents an original initial design.

The floor plan for the traditional Japanese building is known as an *ezuita,* or "plan board," a name derived from the fact that in most cases it was a simple drawing in black ink made on a thin piece of board. Carpenters to this day make similar drawings that show the placement of posts and of such interpost fittings as *fusuma* and *shoji* panels, walls, and *amado* (rain shutters), together with the names of rooms, the types of floor finishings, and the code of joints necessary to guide the builders in the actual assembly of the structure. Among the many such plan boards still extant is the one made by the master carpenter Kawajiri Jisuke for the Kusakabe house, built in 1879 in the city of Takayama in Gifu Prefecture (Figs. 35, 52). It seems miraculous that a house as splendid and complicated as the Kusakabe *minka* could have been built with no other guide at all than this simple plan board.

In the case of the basically simple plans and elevations of temple and shrine architecture, a carpenter with knowledge of certain customary measurements and forms could easily proceed with nothing more than a floor plan of this crude sort. But, aside from some small-scale examples, the *minka* is generally more complicated in plan, and the wishes of the owner tend to influence even small details. Consequently, it seems impossible that such an elaborate building as the Kusakabe house could be built without more explicit written instructions. By all the lights of reason, a three-dimensional building requires the stipulation of dimensions in the vertical direction.

It is here that the carpenter brings his *kenzao,* or measuring rods, into play. These rods are of three varieties: the basic rod (*motozue*), the scale measure (*shakuzue*), and the post (or detail) measure (*hashirazue* or *kanabakarizue*). Carpenters today often use these traditional measuring sticks. The basic rod is marked off in the standard Japanese system of linear measurement and can therefore be used for any building, but it is longer than the usual ruler for convenience in measuring greater distances. The scale measure is marked off in figures that correspond to the scale indicated on the plan board. As a result, it is useful only for the building in question. The detail measure, which performs something like the functions of sectional and elevational drawings, bears markings and positional

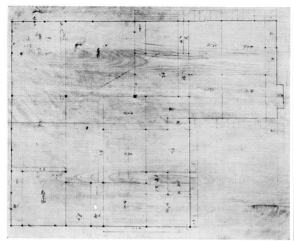

35. Ezuita (plan board) for Kusakabe house in Takayama, Gifu Prefecture, nineteenth century (1879). (See also Figures 37, 44, 52.)

36. Veranda edge and stone for removing footgear. Kita house, nineteenth century, Nonoichi, Ishikawa Prefecture. (See also Figures 8, 42.)

values indicated on the posts. Like the scale measure, it is useful only for the building in question. All measurements of structural materials are made with these guides, and all processing and assembly must follow these measurements.

The plan board and the measuring rods, then, are the basis on which all traditional Japanese buildings—not only the *minka*—are constructed. But from this point on, the *minka* design system diverges from all others.

The placement of the posts is the most important aspect of the floor plan drawn on the plan board. Obviously such placement determines the size, outline, and room division of the building (Figs. 65, 99), but in addition the posts themselves have an even more fundamental meaning—a meaning that becomes easy to understand once the posts are divided into two main categories: primary and secondary. Primary posts are those placed so as to constitute the basic framework. They bear the total load of the building, including that of the roof. The secondary group of posts is composed of those that, from the structural standpoint, have only subordinate importance. Though the secondary posts may be called upon to bear load, their removal will not threaten the structure with collapse. The primary post group is placed in accordance with major structural requirements, the secondary ones in accordance with the functional requirements revealed in the floor plan.

Students of the *minka* frequently have recourse to a reconstruction process in which, by determining the primary posts, they discover how much of the building as it stands dates from the original construction and how much is addition and remodeling from later years. Although it is possible to remove one primary post without incurring immediate total destruction, compensating for the loss of support is generally so troublesome that in virtually all cases remodeling is limited to alterations in the secondary posts, which can be removed or added at will with little effect on the structure. In summary, the primary posts compose the main structural body, while the secondary ones are placed according to functional requirements of the plan.

BASIC STRUCTURES Through the process of creating a reproduction that reveals the placement of the primary posts, one is able to arrive at a picture of the basic structure.

In other words, this process reveals the pattern of post placement automatically dictated by the existence of a certain basic structure. Briefly, to determine the placement of the primary posts is to determine the basic structure of the house. In the *minka* design process it is of the greatest importance that the basic structure be determined before anything else.

In fact, the precedence given the basic structure sharply distinguishes *minka* design from that of the traditional Japanese *sukiya* style and that of the modern functional dwelling, since in the case of the latter styles basic structure is subordinate in importance to the much more vital floor plan. No two types could be more dissimilar than the commonplace present-day house, designed on the premise that the placement of the rooms must be convenient, and the *minka*. Houses built in Japan since the early twentieth century sometimes seem to follow the *minka* tradition when in fact they do not. Most of them employ either the *sukiya* design method or the Western functional method, and many are an unconscious combination of the two. A very few are based on the true *minka* system. One of the most famous of these is the Sky House, designed by Kiyonori Kikutake. It is likely, however, that this building, instead of being a product of the *minka* tradition, is the fruit of Kikutake's own individual philosophy. Nevertheless, I have seen fit to call it *minka* style.

I must say at this point that I am by no means denigrating the important role that functional ideology has played in the modernization of the homes and ways of life of the people. I merely state that from the standpoint of design theory the functional house and the *minka* are two entirely different things.

Of course, the employment of basic structure as the first step in establishing the direction of the design process is common to temple and shrine architecture too, but in such architecture the available basic structures are limited to one general type. The *minka*, on the other hand, can be built around a number of different basic structures. In contrast with conventional shrine and temple architecture, the *minka* basic structure is richly varied, and its

style is free. In the following paragraphs I describe some of the basic *minka* structures (Fig. 41).

1. The inverted U. This most universally applied system, which is seen in buildings of the greatest antiquity, employs a pattern of two posts connected by a beam at their tops. The resulting inverted-U units are joined by side girders. Semantic study of the Japanese words meaning "beam" and "girder" suggests that this structural type is the oldest of all those used in Japan. There are two methods of connecting the posts and beams in this system. In one method, *orioki*, the beam rests directly on the head of the post. This system is used in shrines and temples as well as in *minka*. The other method involves inserting a narrowed section, or tenon, of the end of the beam into a prepared hole, or mortise, in the side of the post and fixing it in place with pins or plugs. This method, called *sashitsuke*, is found only in *minka* and is frequently seen on the side of the island of Shikoku facing the Seto Inland Sea. When the interpost span is great, secondary posts may be used to support the beam in the middle, or the beam may consist of two joined lengths of timber. Houses belonging to the style epitomized by the Hakogi *sennenya* fall into this category. Long-beam versions may be regarded as variations of the basic inverted U. Other variations include arrangements in which the U-shaped units are aligned to form an L plan, a U plan, or a hollow-square plan.

2. The ladder. This framework consists of a number of ladderlike units made up of several posts and beams connected by a number of larger beams. It is thought that the system was first employed in urban houses of the Edo period (1603–1868). Since these dwellings were frequently built tangent to their neighbors with no open space between them, it was difficult to employ the inverted-U structure. The ladder system was devised for the erection of outside walls in such cases. Furthermore, since the system permits irregular placement of posts, it imposes no structural restrictions on the floor plan.

3. The umbrella. From a centrally placed post, beams are cast to form connections with four subordinate posts placed at the middle of each of the four sides of an imaginary square. The system gained its name because the resulting structure

37. Latticework at front of Kusakabe house, nineteenth century (1879), Takayama, Gifu Prefecture. (See also Figures 35, 44, 52.)

38. *Beamwork and hanging shelf over sunken hearth in restored* minka *from Totsugawa, Nara Prefecture, eighteenth century, now in* minka *village, Toyonaka, Osaka Prefecture.*

39. *Earth-floored area (foreground) and* ▷ *entrance to main living quarters, Yoshimura house, seventeenth century, Habikino, Osaka Prefecture. (See also Figures 15, 22, 48, 93, 107, 123.)*

resembles the shaft and ribs of an umbrella. Since the four outer posts are in the centers of the sides and not in the corners of the square, the posts that are later placed in the corners are mere fittings for the sake of the development of walls. The umbrella system is found largely in Shiga Prefecture. Houses using it are called umbrella-style houses, and a view upward into their interior beam structures makes the meaning of the term quite clear.

4. The cross. Two beams joined to form a cross are supported at their ends by four posts. As is the case with the umbrella structure, the posts are placed on the sides of the square formed by the plan, and the corner posts are secondary in importance. Small farmhouses sometimes use only this system and erect no posts within the living space formed by it. Larger *minka,* however, generally use it only in the earth-floored area and employ other systems in the living quarters. The cross system is most common in Shiga and Fukui prefectures.

5. Parallel crosses. A variation of the preceding one, this system consists of two sets of two beams each joined to form two parallel crosses and supported by eight posts at their ends. In the board-roofed *minka* of the Ikawa district of Shizuoka Prefecture, this system is used to cover an area of roughly five by ten meters in the center of which there is a sunken hearth more than one meter to a side.

6. The box. Four or more posts are connected by means of mortised lintels, braces, and beams to create a rigid boxlike framework. The structure is generally used to cover a space roughly six meters to a side. This area may be the earth-floored front part of the house, or it may be the living quarters. In the latter case it may be subdivided into smaller spaces by means of a secondary framework. First devised in the Edo period, the box structure was widely used in *minka* in Toyama and Ishikawa prefectures.

7. The jungle gym. Though the term I have borrowed for this system may be inappropriate in some senses, it seems to suit the appearance of this interconnected group of box structures. High-placed tenon-joint lintels and similar horizontal members bind the posts together. In general, lintels are considered fittings in Japanese architecture, but in cases like this they play important structural roles. The jungle-gym system is found in houses in Kyoto and Osaka, but the names for the structural elements used in that region vary from the names used elsewhere. Interestingly enough, the names of these elements sometimes change from place to place within a single house.

8. Rising beams. Devised to enhance the usability of second-floor atticlike rooms, this system is employed in two-story warehouses all over the country and is especially common in urban houses in the Sanyo district of western Honshu. The houses in the famous city of Kurashiki, for example, are almost all of this system (Fig. 53). The side posts are connected by means of the second-story girders and the end posts by means of girders placed on their heads. From each girder rises a slanting beam that rests at the top on a secondary ridge installed superficially to support it. The true ridge rests in the crotches formed by the projections of the slanting beams. Also from the slanting beams project struts that in turn support the purlins on which the rafters rest. Since this system employs no horizontal upper beams, it makes possible the advantageous use of second-story space.

In concluding my remarks about basic structures I must point out that the ones I have discussed are only a few garnered from the Kinki, Hokuriku, Sanyo, and Tokai regions of Japan. There are many more. In fact, it might well be that specific kinds of basic structures are important regional characteristics of the *minka*.

Also, I should like to stress once again the fact

40. Beamwork in Imanishi house, seventeenth century (1650), Imai-cho, Kashihara, Nara Prefecture. (See also Figures 5, 46, 67, 74.)

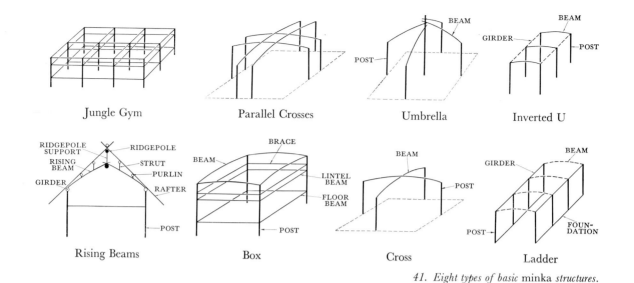

Jungle Gym

Parallel Crosses

Umbrella

Inverted U

Rising Beams

Box

Cross

Ladder

41. Eight types of basic minka *structures.*

42. Beamwork in Kita house, nineteenth century, Nonoichi, Ishikawa Prefecture. (See also Figures 8, 36.)

43. Beamwork and smoke vent, Nagatomi house, nineteenth century (1820), Ibogawa, Hyogo Prefecture. (See also Figures 45, 78, 96, 103.)

44. Living room, Kusakabe house, nineteenth century (1879), Takayama, Gifu Prefecture. (See also Figures 35, 37, 52.)

45. *Beamwork in Nagatomi house, nineteenth century (1820), Ibogawa, Hyogo Prefecture. (See also Figures 43, 78, 96, 103.)*

46. *Second-floor guest room, Imanishi house, seventeenth century (1650), Imai-cho, Kashihara, Nara Prefecture. (See also Figures 5, 40, 67, 74.)*

that the *minka* design is based more on basic structure than on a functional floor plan. By this, I do not imply that functional planning is totally overlooked. I merely insist that such planning is limited to the level of secondary structure and fittings. *Minka* are all built of wood. Were they built of steel and concrete and under modern systems of dynamics to suit the demands of modern living, they would doubtless require other kinds of basic structures.

THE POST AS SYMBOL   The placement of the primary structural posts so clearly symbolizes the basic structure itself that research workers experienced in *minka* methods can mentally determine the latter by merely examining the former. The combination of the pri-

mary and secondary posts, then, symbolizes the entire framework of the building, and from the standpoint of dynamics these posts bear the entire load of the house. But from the standpoint of total design, even when the *minka* framework is complete, the floor plan is not established until the fittings—floors, ceilings, walls, and partitions—have been installed. The basic structural posts, once in place, cannot be moved, no matter whether they suit the floor-plan requirements or run contrary to them. The secondary posts, however, fall outside this discussion because they are placed in accordance with the floor plan. Therefore the primary structure may be regarded in two lights: it may be considered a restriction of freedom in designing floor plans, or it may be thought of as the basic network that gives direction to the floor plan. In short, in addition to

47. *Detail of eaves, Kamikura house, nineteenth century, Machida, Tokyo Prefecture. (See also Figure 57.)*

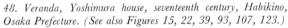

48. *Veranda, Yoshimura house, seventeenth century, Habikino, Osaka Prefecture. (See also Figures 15, 22, 39, 93, 107, 123.)*

49. *Natural log used as main supporting pillar in Kono house, eighteenth century, Enzan, Yamanashi Prefecture. (See also Figure 64.)*

its function in dynamics as a load bearer, the primary structure serves to order the building's spaces and roughly to outline the plan. Consequently, when viewed in this light, the selection of basic structures for *minka* takes on added importance.

To talk of the space around a single column perhaps makes sense in poetry but not in practical theory, since a space must be bounded by some physical limitation. Nevertheless, the notion that a single post is surrounded by a certain space rings true in a literary sense because it is possible to imagine such a space even if not to see it. This notion, in turn, clearly reveals the spatial symbolism. The sacred posts at the famous Kasuga Shrine in Nara and at the Iwashimizu Hachiman Shrine in Kyoto Prefecture are symbols of deities, and therefore people never approach them too closely for fear of divine retribution. The Japanese often use the word *ma* to express the kind of abstract space symbolized by the single post. The primary posts of a *minka* symbolize the *ma*, or abstract space, of the building, and the secondary posts and related fittings give that space visual form (Fig. 99). Modern architects, though their viewpoints vary slightly from this, observe the *minka* in the light of a basic structure symbolizing and ordering space.

FUNCTIONAL DURABILITY   In the overwhelming majority of cases, during their long lifetimes, *minka* undergo repairs and alterations extending to exterior appearance, floor plans, and all kinds of details. The very fact that in the process of repairing *minka* that have been designated important cultural

50. *Guest room in Oya house, eighteenth century, Kawachi Nagano, Osaka Prefecture. (See also Figure 51.)*

51. *Lattice-enclosed veranda of* ▷ *Oya house, eighteenth century, Kawachi Nagano, Osaka Prefecture. (See also Figure 50.)*

properties it is felt necessary to restore the building to original form underscores the importance of the many changes that take place in these houses. In general, such changes affect only the secondary structure and the fittings. In other words, as functional requirements alter, it is possible to conform the *minka* to the needs of any given historical period by simply adjusting the secondary structure and fittings. Throughout history, family compositions change, living styles alter, and things in fashion at one time are replaced by newer things. These changes naturally work alterations in the functional demands made on a building. Of course, the *minka* is not the only architectural style that can conform to changes in a flexible manner. Shrine and temple architecture also has this capability, but, since religious architecture is basically conservative, efforts are usually expended to preserve the old or original appearances of such structures. In comparison, the *minka* is much more free and versatile.

In the clumsy and often ugly distorted shapes resulting from rebuilding and altering *minka*, it is possible to discern a certain development order. Although the primary structure does not change, one can conform the house to the functional needs of the times by altering the exterior, the floor plan, and the details. This means that, within the limits imposed by the immutable basic structure, it is possible to develop all kinds of irregular forms. The *minka* design system is based on the premise that functional requirements change constantly, and for this reason it inherently contains the possibility of various external forms. A single structural system, then, allows the production of exteriors that, at a glance, seem to be the diametric opposite of what one might expect from such a system. The concept on which this system is based is Oriental and fundamentally Buddhist. We people of the Orient are mentally attracted to both static geometric beauty and to a kind of processing, altering order of

beauty represented by the *minka*. A young foreign architect of my acquaintance once found what he called wonderful hints in the grotesquely bulging and receding lines of a much-altered *minka*. I do not think that the *minka* exists primarily to serve as a source of useful information, but it is certainly true that architects today, paying attention to things that designers of the past overlooked, can derive a number of good lessons from the *minka* design system.

THE AREA UNDER THE EAVES In comparison not only with those of Western houses but also with those of contemporary Japanese residential architecture, the roofs of the *minka* are very large. Furthermore, the influence of the roof on the *minka* is very great. One of the primary reasons for the mammoth scale of *minka* roofs is their importance as a symbol of status in the society of the village or the town. A document called the *Kasuga-jinja Monjo,* dating from the Muromachi period, says that the length of the ridgepole of a house indicated the position and status of the occupant and that taxes were levied in accordance with this length. Generally speaking, in feudal Japan wealth and position were parallel. That is to say, length of ridgepole, size of house, and size of roof indicated both the money required to construct them and the social position of the owner. In the Edo period, however, the number of ornaments on the ridgepole signified the standing of the family. For instance, during this period, in the Kamiminochi district of Nagano Prefecture, houses whose owners were of a status too low to permit them to wear the short outer garment called the *haori* were limited to no more than three ornaments on the ridgepole. A family of somewhat higher standing might display five, and a household of good position might indulge itself in as many as seven or nine. Similar examples of architectural

52. Front view of Kusakabe house, nineteenth century (1879), Takayama, Gifu Prefecture. (See also Figures 35, 37, 44.)

53. Urban houses in Kurashiki, Okayama Prefecture.

54. *Front view of Furuhata house, nineteenth century, Hongo Village, Nagano Prefecture.*

55. Side view of Hori house, said to date from the fourteenth or fifteenth century, Nishi Yoshino Village, Nara Prefecture. (See also Figure 82.)

56. *Urban house in Kamioka, Gifu Prefecture.*

57. Front view of Kamikura house, nineteenth century, Machida, Tokyo Prefecture. (See also Figure 47.)

58. *Inokuma house and outbuildings, nineteenth century, Shirotori, Kagawa Prefecture.*

60. Front view of Yamada house and storehouses, eighteenth century, Kyoto.

61. Urban houses in Kamioka, Gifu Prefecture.

◁ *59. Izumo-style* minka, *nineteenth century, Hirata, Shimane Prefecture.*

63 (opposite page, top). Guest ▷
room in Toshima house, seventeenth
century, Ukiana Village, Ehime
Prefecture. (See also Figures 80,
99.)

64 (opposite page, bottom). Attic ▷
of Kono house, eighteenth century,
Enzan, Yamanashi Prefecture. (See
also Figure 49.)

62. Board floored veranda and earth-floored area under eaves, Nara house, eighteenth
century (1764), Akita City, Akita Prefecture. (See also Figures 72, 104, 105.)

elements serving as visual symbols of the feudal
social structure could be cited from all over Japan.

The second important reason for the size of the
minka roof is a functional one. In Japan, where
driving rains are frequent, deep eaves protect the
interior. In addition, since yearly typhoons bring
great downpours, a steep roof pitch helps to prevent
leakage. Although sliding rain shutters might provide similar indoor protection even without deep
eaves, the darkness and the high humidity caused
by closing the shutters would be intolerable for any
protracted period. Moreover, deep eaves shut out
the singeing rays of the high summer sun and yet
allow the warming light of the lower winter sun to
penetrate into the rooms. Today, of course, with
mechanical means of controlling indoor conditions,
it is no longer essential to pay a great deal of attention to the overhang of the eaves.

The necessity of creating a status symbol and a
means of controlling indoor climate inevitably gave
birth to the heavy roof with deep eaves. This in turn
created an area under the eaves: the *nokishita,* as
the Japanese call it (Fig. 47). The fact that in order
to express this space one must resort to as awkward
a phrase as "area under the eaves" indicates the
non-Occidental nature of the thing itself.

Often there is a veranda (*engawa*) in the area
under the eaves (Figs. 48, 51, 62). Sometimes the
veranda is left open to the elements, and sometimes
it is closed at its outer edge with rain shutters,
translucent sliding panels of wood and paper
(*shoji*), or glazed sliding doors. In general, the eaves
project only slightly beyond the veranda, although
in the far north, where heavy snows are frequent,
beyond the wooden-floored veranda there is a lower
area floored with pounded earth and protected

65. Guest room in Yagumo honjin, *formerly an inn for daimyo, eighteenth century, Shinji, Shimane Prefecture. (See also Figures 34, 89, 97.)*

from the weather by means of shutters with glass windows in their upper sections. This device both protects the interior from in-blowing snow and provides sufficient indoor lighting. In these cases the eaves must be deep enough to cover the earth-floored zone and to project slightly beyond it. The nature of the veranda is a dual one. Located beyond the exterior walls of the house, it is naturally outdoor space, and yet, since its wooden floor is in a sense an extension of the interior floors, it is also a part of the indoors. In fact, a number of indoor daily-life activities are performed in this space.

If, on the other hand, instead of being occupied by a wooden-floored veranda, the area under the eaves were outfitted with nothing more than stepping-stones, it would clearly be completely exterior in nature. In contrast with architectural parlance,

Japanese garden terminology generally refers to this zone as exterior. In a word, architects think of the space as interior, while landscape gardeners treat it as exterior.

The area under the eaves, then, partakes of the natures of both interior and exterior without strictly being a part of either. To the Western mind, for which a thing must usually be either A or B, a space that is at once two things without being either is a vague and difficult concept. That concept, however, not only exists but also finds visual form in the architectural device of the area under the eaves.

Viewed from another standpoint, this apparently vague area under the eaves is the junction zone at which the interior, or architectural, spaces and the exterior spaces of nature come together. Although the interpenetration of interior and exterior is not a

66. *View of stable, Chiba house, nineteenth century (1830), Ayaori, Tono, Iwate Prefecture. (See also Figure 128.)*

visible thing, a person sitting in this region experiences the combination physically. The nature of the area under the eaves is of the greatest importance to the well-known intimacy maintained between Japanese architectural spaces and nature.

The tendency of the area under the eaves to effect a junction between two zones is interestingly pointed up in the case of two adjacent houses. If the eaves of the two houses come close to each other, although the interior spaces of the two preserve physical independence, one has the impression that the area under the eaves connects the buildings. In other words, although this space involves physical separation, it makes possible mutual spatial interpenetration.

The use of this space to evoke a feeling of union with nature is not truly ancient in the history of Japanese architecture. For example, in the pit dwellings common in Japan in the paleolithic and neolithic ages and even into early historical times, the roof extended to ground level, and there was no area under the eaves at all (Fig. 135). The lack of a zone of junction between interior and exterior suggests that in these times the world of nature was considered an inimical force. We do not have sufficient historical data to determine when large openings, peripheral posts, and the resultant area under the eaves made their several appearances in residential buildings, but the presence of a veranda in the now vanished Rin'ami house, which was built in Kyoto in 1397, makes it possible to assume that at least in certain kinds of *minka* the transition had been made by the early years of the Muromachi period.

CHAPTER THREE

The Development of Special Minka Characteristics

REGIONAL TRAITS AND SOCIAL SYMBOLISM   Anyone who knows anything about the *minka* will immediately place its local traits at the top of the list of its special characteristics. This is not to imply that such local color is totally absent from such other important branches of Japanese architecture as shrine and temple buildings. It is true that in regions of heavy snowfall there is less use of shingle roofs for temples because the bamboo nails required to hold the shingles in place rot very quckly. Details in provincial temple and shrine buildings are often considerably less refined than those found in buildings in Kyoto, and there are examples of strictly local architectural elements like the lintel style found only in Saga Prefecture. Nevertheless, these local characteristics, when compared with the radical differences found among *minka* of various regions, are of such slight importance that they may be overlooked.

At this point it is important to emphasize another aspect of the local characteristics of *minka*. These traits are by no means entirely dependent on geographical distribution. In fact, there are often two or three kinds of geographical distribution that vary according to one's interpretation of the traits themselves. Consequently, a given *minka* is frequently a compound of traits from a number of

localities. This is probably a result of the long historical process by means of which the *minka* has developed. I shall give a few examples of this phenomenon in a later section of the present discussion.

As might be expected in the light of the long history of the *minka*, architectural characteristics tend to alter with the historical period as well as the locality. It is now very difficult to find *minka* authentically dating from earlier than the Genroku era (1688–1704), which is thought to have been a great age of alteration in *minka* styles. For instance, the appearances of the ordinary urban houses of that time in the Kinki district offer no hint of the *chodai* —a board-walled room provided with ornamental sliding doors on one side—that was among the most important inner rooms of this kind of house before the Genroku era. We know that the Imanishi, Shijo, and Toyota houses in Kashihara, Nara Prefecture, had this architectural feature. In fact, a *chodai* room remains today in the Imanishi residence. All these houses were built between 1650 and 1667. Other evidence of great change in *minka* and rural-living styles during the second half of the seventeenth century can be found in a book called *Seidan*, written by the distinguished philosopher and scholar Ogyu Sorai, in which it is stated that until the Genroku era farmers drank a thick, unrefined

67. *Gables of Imanishi house, seventeenth century (1650), Imai-cho, Kashihara, Nara Prejecture. (See also Figures 5, 40, 46, 74.)*

saké called *doburoku,* wore nothing but cotton, and slept on straw matting, whereas townsmen enjoyed luxuries unknown to their country cousins—for example, sliding interior partitions (*fusuma*), ceilings, patterned *fusuma* paper, *tatami* mats, and mosquito nets. All of this indicates the extent to which architecture and daily life were changing in the late seventeenth and early eighteenth centuries. Since one can readily assume from such facts that local *minka* characteristics were also changing around the same time, it is dangerous to conclude unconditionally that the geographic distribution of characterizing architectural features as they exist today represents conditions prevailing in earlier historical periods.

A second general important trait of the *minka* is its nature as physical symbolization of the class order of Japanese feudal society. Since it developed over an eight-century span in which feudalism was the nation's way of life, the *minka* could scarcely fail to manifest the social structure. Such things as size, length of span, number of ridgepole ornaments (Fig. 120), and the presence or absence of such features as gatehouses (Fig. 78), *genkan* entryways (Fig. 87), tokonoma alcove and adjacent ornamental shelves (Fig. 63, right), ceilings, decorative horizontal members called *nageshi*, and, in rarer cases, of outbuildings, peripheral verandas, and inner gates—all these told at a glance whether the occupant was a government official in a town or a village, whether he was a landowner or a tenant farmer, and more or less where he stood in the urban or rural social scale. Although in later ages, as the feudal system began to crumble and as the government imposed various sumptuary restrictions on buildings, many of the social symbols in *minka* tended to lose significance, in general they remained a revealing guide to social status.

Whereas size, number of ornaments, and the presence of certain dignifying architectural ap-

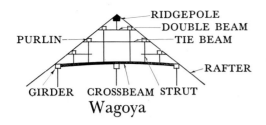

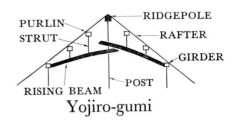

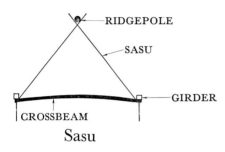

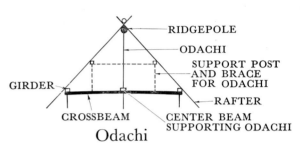

68. Roof-truss structures. Top to bottom, left to right: wagoya, yojiro-gumi, sasu, odachi.

purtenances indicated the status of the owner, certain interior conventions went further to indicate the social relationships among people living in a given house at a given time. For instance, only the most elevated personages present were allowed to sit in the so-called *jodan,* or raised and *tatami*-covered section of the inner room of the house. Those slightly less lofty in comparative rank might sit on the lower wooden-floored section, and the lowliest were confined to the earth-floored *doma.* In addition, just as one's position relative to the saltcellar at formal Western banquets once indicated the esteem in which one was held by the host, so in the formal Japanese sitting room the most favored guests are seated closer to the post (*tokobashira*) that forms the most obvious structural feature of the ornamental alcove, the tokonoma.

The third characterizing trait of the *minka* in general is the nature of the materials employed in its construction. Although stone and tile were sometimes used, the predominant material was wood, and the leading secondary materials were grass thatch and clay. None of these are materials suited to society today. Wood, of course, burns easily, but not so easily as grass thatch. In the past, miscanthus rushes were employed in roofing, but they are now extremely difficult to obtain. Finally, clay walls are brittle, and they crumble easily.

All three of the foregoing major characteristics, then, ill suit the *minka* to modern society, and in a sense this is the tragedy of this architectural type. Nevertheless, the study of the *minka* throws the light of a new interpretation on many aspects of the tradition and lineage of Japanese culture. Unfortunately, the still immature stage of this study does not permit maximum use of the suggestions the *minka* can make concerning history and tradition, but in this book I hope to make a contribution to the furthering of the general effort in this line.

ROOF-TRUSS STRUCTURES For the sake of this discussion the roof truss is the structure above the main beams, or the part of the structure that appears to be triangular when seen in cross section. The so-called Japanese truss (*wagoya*), or a simplification of it, is most often

69. *Front view of* gassho-*style farmhouse, nineteenth century, Kamitaira Village, Toyama Prefecture.*

70. *Front view of Asa house, eighteenth century, Higashi Iyayama Village, Tokushima Prefecture.*

71. Front view of Kodera house, nineteenth century, Kiyose, Tokyo Prefecture.

72. Chumon *section of Nara house, eighteenth century (1764), Koizumi, Akita City, Akita Prefecture. (See also Figures 62, 104, 105.)*

73. Naka house, seventeenth century, Kumatori, Osaka Prefecture. (See also Figures 19, 87.)

74. *Exterior detail of Imanishi house, built by a former samurai family, seventeenth century (1650), Imai-cho, Kashihara, Nara Prefecture. (See also Figures 5, 40, 46, 67.)*

76. *Attic of Shirakawa house in* gassho *style, eighteenth century, min-ka village, Toyonaka, Osaka Prefecture.*

77. *Detail of eaves and clay wall, Toyota house, seventeenth century, Kashihara, Nara Prefecture.*

used with tiled roofs, but since neither it nor the tile roof was employed in Japan until the introduction of Buddhist architecture in the sixth century, the *wagoya* must be excluded from discussions of truly primitive *minka*. I shall deal only with the kinds of trusses used with thatched roofs, and from that general category I shall omit the so-called town *minka* that was first widely popular in the Heian period. In short, I shall deal only with those roof-truss structures found in grass-thatched rural *minka*.

Roof trusses for houses of this type fall into four general categories (Fig. 68). The first, also called *wagoya* (Japanese truss), is based on the above-noted *wagoya* used for tile roofs. It occurs with great rarity, but examples are to be found in the kitchen

of the Egawa house at Nirayama in Shizuoka Prefecture (Fig. 145) and in the Shinke house in Inatsu, Okayama Prefecture. The second style, the *yojiro-gumi* truss, though somewhat more widely used than the one just mentioned, is nonetheless uncommon and is not sufficiently widespread to be a local characteristic of any particular region. Some say that the name of the style derives from that of an Edo-period criminal who is supposed to have devised the structure; others maintain that the name is a corruption of that of a famous toy called the *yajirobe*.

The two remaining truss styles, the *sasu* and the *odachi*, are prevalent enough to be called local characteristics. The *sasu* style, the most common throughout Japan, consists of a ridgepole supported

◁ 75. *Storehouse (*kura*), nineteenth century, Kurashiki, Okayama Prefecture.*

78 (*opposite page, top*). *Gatehouse, Nagatomi house, nineteenth century (1820), Ibogawa, Hyogo Prefecture. (See also Figures 43, 45, 96, 103.)*

79 (*opposite page, bottom*). *Front view of Nishio house, eighteenth century, Tottori City, Tottori Prefecture.*

80 (*top*). *Toshima house and outbuildings, seventeenth century, Ukiana Village, Ehime Prefecture. (See also Figures 63, 99.)*

81 (*right*). Segaı *eaves structure, Shioda house, nineteenth century, Nio, Kagawa Prefecture.*

82. *Front view of Hori house, said to date from the fourteenth or fifteenth century, Nishi Yoshino Village, Nara Prefecture. (See also Figure 55.)*

on two rising slanting members (*sasu*). The *odachi* style, most common in the Kinki (Kyoto-Osaka) region, employs short vertical posts to support the ridgepole. The word *odachi* is a local term for such posts.

For a long time all except a very few specialists insisted that thatched roofs invariably used the *sasu* system, but in a collection of plans of *minka* architecture, *Nihon Minka Kenchiku Zushu*, Kenji Ishihara points out that houses in the Tamba district of Kyoto use not the *sasu* but the *odachi* system. Initially his thesis met much opposition, but about ten years ago it was conclusively proved that the *odachi* system is used in most *minka* of the Osaka-Kyoto area. Although it is true that the *sasu* system is prevalent in modern *minka* of the Kyoto area, the fact that the *odachi* system persists in the older *minka* of Tamba and in other parts of this region suggests

that in the distant past it was universally used and that at some time (probably during the Edo period) a shift was made to the *sasu* system. In other words, at least until the end of the Muromachi period, the *odachi* was the common structure.

A genre of pictures and screens called *Rakuchu Rakugai Zu* (Scenes in and Around Kyoto) offers very valuable information on the nature of the houses of the sixteenth and seventeenth centuries. For instance, a famous pair of *Rakuchu Rakugai* six-panel screens painted in the early sixteenth century and now owned by the Machida family of Tokyo show houses of town and country and offer an interesting hint about the possible prototype of the *odachi* structural system. One of the urban houses depicted has a board roof and a ridgepole supported at either end by free-standing posts of the kind found at both the Ise and the Izumo shrines. Since

83. Tamba-style minka, *Wachi, Kyoto Prefecture.*

84. Front view of minka *with* sasu *roof-truss structure, nineteenth century, Takachiho, Miyazaki Prefecture.*

the drawing shows no internal beams and is therefore extremely dubious as material for structural analysis, it is likely that it is no more than an artist's fiction. Nevertheless, it is possible that this kind of structure still existed in the Muromachi period, when houses were still small. Furthermore, since the ridge is supported on vertical elements, just as is the case with the *odachi*, it may be that this is the original form from which the style evolved.

In the southern part of Wakayama Prefecture the *odachi* is most generally used, and the *sennenya*, the thousand-year houses, thought to have been built in the Muromachi period, endorse the idea that the *odachi* style was prevalent in the past in the eastern part of Hyogo Prefecture. Even today this style persists in many of houses in the Nosè region of Osaka Prefecture (Fig. 126), near both the Kyoto district of Tamba and Hyogo Prefecture. Although

the structural system used in houses in Mie and Shiga prefectures is uncertain, the use, in a Muromachi-period set of tax regulations, of words suggesting posts supporting the ridgepole makes it seem likely that, at any rate, the basic structural system in these prefectures in the past did not employ slanting members of the *sasu* type.

No matter what the prevailing conditions in outlying regions, however, the possibility is great that in Kyoto the *odachi* was most frequent. In fact, Kyoto was probably the center from which the system was propagated. I must make it clear, however, that houses in the Kyoto-Nara region today employ mainly the *sasu* style and that *odachi*-system houses surround this center in a kind of doughnut fashion. But the *sasu* system developed in the central zone and thus gave rise to the doughnut phenomenon no earlier than the Edo period.

85. *Front view of Ozaki house, which has a* sasu *roof-truss structure, eighteenth century, Hawai, Tottori Prefecture.* (*See also Figures 90, 124.*)

Although one can tell that the *odachi* held the upper hand as late as the Muromachi period, it is less easy to ascertain the other end of the historical scale—that is, the point in time when the system gained prevalence—because research data on this matter is sadly lacking. If one can assume that the *odachi* style existed in the Kyoto district as early as the age of pit dwellings, clearly the placement of the holes for these dwellings found in the remains in the Kyoto area would differ sharply from the placement found in other locations. But unfortunately on this issue, too, evidence is not forthcoming.

It is possible, however, to pin down the spread of the style within certain broad limits by means of applying two reasonable assumptions. First, since the *odachi* system is distributed largely in the area of the ancient urban centers of Japan—Kyoto, Nara, and Osaka—its development probably took place

after the national cultural center shifted from northern Kyushu to this zone, which is traditionally called Yamato. That is to say, the style in all likelihood evolved after the beginning of the Yayoi period (200 B.C. to A.D. 250). On the basis of distribution it is difficult to assign its initial stages to the preceding Jomon period.

But distribution is not the only point in support of this dating, for the tenons and mortises absolutely essential to the *odachi* system require iron tools, and the Jomon age knew no such implements. (I must note here, however, that it is possible to effect something like the true *odachi* by using branches with Y-shaped ends.) The *sasu* structural type, on the other hand, does not require tenons and mortises, although in modern versions these devices have been found advantageous.

Since the ancient historical chronicles *Kojiki*

86. Front view of Yamamura house, nineteenth century, Sonobe, Kyoto Prefecture.

87. Front view of Naka house, seventeenth century, Kumatori, Osaka Prefecture. (See also Figures 19, 73.)

88. Misegura *(shop-storehouse), nineteenth century, Kawagoe, Saitama Prefecture.*

89. Lattice door and transom of Yagumo honjin, *formerly an inn for daimyo, eighteenth century, Shinji, Shimane Prefecture. (See also Figures 34, 65, 97.)*

90. View of earth-floored area and sliding doors, Ozaki house, eighteenth century, Hawai, Tottori Prefecture. (See also Figures 85, 124.)

91. *Front view of main shop of Wachu-san, a firm dealing in Chinese medicines, seventeenth century, Ritto, Shiga Prefecture. (See also Figure 114.)*

92. *Section of main living quarters of Yoshijima house, twentieth century, Taka-yama, Gifu Prefecture.*

94. *Beamwork in Kuriyama house, seventeenth century (1607), Gojo, Nara Prefecture. (See also Figure 152.)*

◁ 93. *Main entrance to Yoshimura house, seventeenth century, Habikino, Osaka Prefecture.*
(See also Figures 15, 22, 39, 48, 107, 123.)

95. *Socket hinge on door of clay-plastered storehouse of Omiya shop, nineteenth century, Yamagata City, Yamagata Prefecture. (See also Figure 10.)*

96. Guest rooms in Nagatomi house, nineteenth century (1820), Ibogawa, Hyogo Prefecture. (See also Figures 43, 45, 78, 103.)

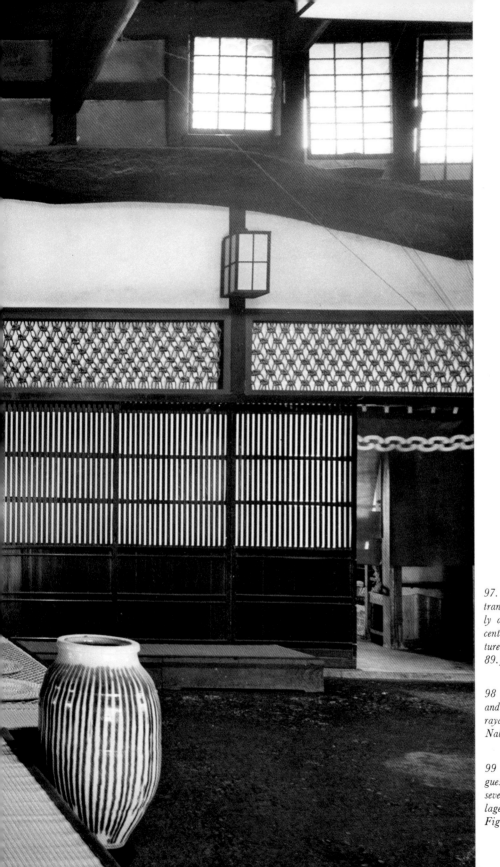

97. Earth-floored area and entrance to Yagumo honjin, formerly an inn for daimyo, eighteenth century, Shinji, Shimane Prefecture. (See also Figures 34, 65, 89.)

98 (overleaf, left). Guest rooms ▷ and earth-floored section of Tawaraya inn, eighteenth century, Nabari, Mie Prefecture.

99 (overleaf, right). Detail of ▷ guest room in Toshima house, seventeenth century, Ukiana Village, Ehime Prefecture. (See also Figures 63, 80.)

100. Earth-floored area of Horiuchi house, eighteenth century, Shiojiri, Nagano Prefecture. (See also Figures 20, 108, 121.)

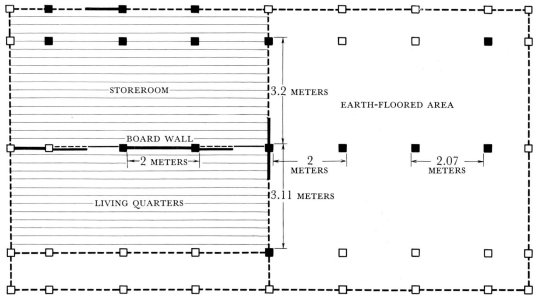

STOREROOM

3.2 METERS

EARTH-FLOORED AREA

BOARD WALL

2 METERS

2 METERS

2.07 METERS

LIVING QUARTERS

3.11 METERS

101. Floor plan of Furui sennenya *(thousand-year house), probably fifteenth or sixteenth century, Antomi, Hyogo Prefecture.*

(Records of Ancient Matters) and *Nihon Shoki* (History of Japan) both mention the word *sasu*, it is entirely reasonable to assume that this structural system existed in the Kinki district during the Tumulus period (250–552). Still, the presence of ridge-supporting posts in both the Ise and the Izumo shrines—located some distance from the Kinki district and both based on styles typical of the Tumulus period—suggests either that during the same age structures employing both vertical supports and slanting ones existed side by side or that there was another structural system amounting to a composite of the two.

Still another line of thought assists one in placing the *odachi* in proper historical perspective. Since the *odachi* system uses vertical supports and is therefore based on the same general principle as the *wagoya*, the so-called Japanese-style system, some specialists hold that it developed and fell under the influence of the *wagoya* after it was first put to use in Buddhist buildings. If this is the case, the *odachi* system must

date from before the Asuka period (552–646), when Buddhism and its culture were introduced into Japan.

Finally, common sense about structural strength lends further credibility to the advanced age of the *odachi* system. Obviously the *sasu* system is more rigid than the *odachi*. The structures of the thousand-year houses make this sufficiently plain. Posts supporting the ridge rest on crossbeams but must be reinforced by means of long braces. In the Hakogi *sennenya* further slender braces are required, although this was not the case in the now lost Sakata *sennenya*. Furthermore, in the northern Tamba district the ridge-supporting posts must be reinforced by means of additional bracing posts called *torii*, presumably from their resemblance to the ceremonial Shinto-shrine gateways of the same name. Probably the Edo-period shift from *odachi* to *sasu* took place in the Kyoto vicinity because of the structural weakness of the former. Since positing a course of development whereby the *minka* structures

102. *Earth-floored area of Abumiya inn, eighteenth century, Sakata, Yamagata Prefecture.*

103. *Front view of Nagatomi house, nineteenth century, Ibogawa, Hyogo Prefecture. This house uses the* tatami *as a basic module. (See also Figures 43, 45, 78, 96.)*

104. Side view of Nara house, eighteenth century (1764), Akita City, Akita Prefecture. This house uses the interpost span as a basic module. (See also Figures 62, 72, 105.)

105. Interior view of Nara house, eighteenth century (1764), Akita City, Akita Prefecture. (See also Figures 62, 72, 104.)

106. Minka *with* kabuto yane *(helmet roofs)*, *Tamugimata, Asahi Village, Yamagata Prefecture. These houses use the interpost span as a basic module.*

107. Shoin-style room with tokonoma and shoin *window alcove, Yoshimura house, seventeenth century, Habikino, Osaka Prefecture. (See also Figures 15, 22, 39, 48, 93, 123.)*

in this zone changed once from *sasu* to *odachi* and then in the Edo period went back again to *sasu* runs counter to good reason, in all likelihood the *odachi* system is at least as old as the Tumulus period and may be older.

THE INFLUENCE OF ROOF STRUCTURES ON FLOOR PLANS In the preceding section I have spent some time on the question of the local distribution of the *odachi* and *sasu* structural systems, not only because the two are themselves intrinsically different but also because they exert strong influence on floor plans. The *odachi* invariably involves a row of posts placed along the center line of the house and directly under the ridgepole. In the past it may have been that the ridge-supporting posts extended from

the roof all the way to the ground under the house, but in later *minka* the ridge supports are small posts resting on beams. In order to enable these supports to bear the load of the ridge, however, it is imperative to place a row of posts under the beams on which they rest. This row of posts obviously runs down the center line of the house. Interpost measurements vary from case to case. In the *minka* of the Tamba district this span is two *ken*, or somewhat less than four meters. In the Furui *sennenya* in the town of Antomi, Hyogo Prefecture, however, the posts are a regular *ken* (nearly two meters) apart and are placed throughout both the living spaces and the earth-floored area (Fig. 101). This is somewhat unusual, since the use of posts in the earth-floored area tends to limit its functional efficiency. For this reason, posts on the center line are usually

108. *Front view of Horiuchi house, eighteenth century, Shiojiri, Nagano Prefecture. This house uses the interpost span as a basic module. (See also Figures 20, 100, 121.)*

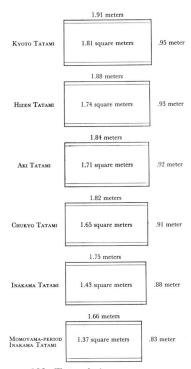

109. Tatami *sizes.*

omitted in this area, and a special beam structure is employed to carry the load of the upper structure. Interestingly enough, a center line of posts (about four meters apart) in the oldest extant *minka* floor plan, that of the previously noted Rin'ami house at the Uematsu manor, strengthens the possibility that though the roof here employed the *sasu* system it was originally designed to use the *odachi* structure.

All of this aside, however, in general the necessity of this central line of posts inevitably means that the *odachi* structural system imposes restrictions on the floor plan. In addition, since these posts are truly structural and thus cannot be moved or removed, they must be used for purposes of partitioning. In the tradition of the *sennenya* the line of posts becomes the dividing line between the storage room and the living space (*hiroshiki*). When the entrance of the house is on the long side—as is the case with

most of these houses—the two rooms are aligned one in front of the other. In the houses of the Nosè section of Osaka and of the neighboring Tamba district (Fig. 83), on the other hand, the entrance is on the gable end, and either the left or the right side becomes the earth-floored part of the house. The remaining side is used as the living area. Houses of this style, while they are farmhouses in a very real sense, differ little in plan from town houses.

In contrast with the *odachi* system, the *sasu* system exerts little direct influence on the internal floor plan, for the slanting beams that form the basis of the structure are supported at their lower ends by the beams (in some newer *minka* by crossbeams). Although this affects the placement of the peripheral side posts, it does not impose the necessity of installing structural posts at particular places in

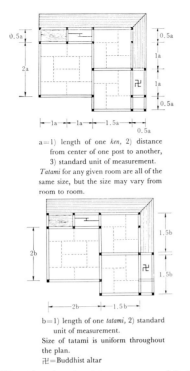

a=1) length of one *ken*, 2) distance from center of one post to another, 3) standard unit of measurement.
Tatami for any given room are all of the same size, but the size may vary from room to room.

b=1) length of one *tatami*, 2) standard unit of measurement.
Size of tatami is uniform throughout the plan.
卍=Buddhist altar

110. *Floor plans based on interpost-span module (top) and* tatami *module (bottom).*

111. *Front view of Ohara house, nineteenth century, Kurashiki, Okayama Prefecture. This house uses the* tatami *as a basic module.*

the plan. Consequently, the *sasu* system leaves the plan more unobstructed than the *odachi* system does.

The now lost Jitogata Mandokoro in Niimi, Okayama Prefecture, thought to have been built in 1463 and once the residence of a farmer-samurai, lacked a central line of posts and therefore could not have had an *odachi* upper structural system. If, as is true at present, only these two kinds of structural systems are conceivable, this house (Fig. 150) almost certainly employed the *sasu* method.

Consequently, one can surmise that in the fourteenth and fifteenth centuries, though the *odachi* was prevalent in Kyoto and its environs, the *sasu* was being used in the city of Niimi in Okayama Prefecture. One point of view holds that it may be dangerous to make such a generalization on the basis of two isolated cases, since specially recorded houses like these are described and recorded precisely because there is something special about them. Still, since in many cases the *minka* developed in isolated local areas and under conditions of communal labor by rural people linked with strong localized ways of thinking and working, it is probably still less reasonable to assume that people from the same district would alter the truss structures to which they had become accustomed unless they had some good reason for doing so.

As the two distinct floor-plan systems inevitably imposed by the two different truss systems developed, both came to employ four-room divisions so similar that the nature of the truss gradually ceased to be a problem. Furthermore, variations in mainbeam and second-story-beam arrangements liberated to some extent even the *odachi* by making it possible to eliminate some (usually only one or two) of the central line of posts under the ridge.

112. *Front view of Kobaien, a shop specializing in ink sticks, nineteenth century, Nara City, Nara Prefecture. (See also Figure 115.)*

MODULE BASED ON TATAMI OR INTERPOST SPAN

The *tatami*, a mat made of rushes with a fine upper layer woven of a grass called *igusa*, serves as a kind of floor-plan module when made in one standard size. In the case of a *minka*, if there are no central posts, not only the *tatami* but also the sliding doors and partitions (*shoji* and *fusuma*) may be based on a standard size, thus increasing convenience in building. The area around Kyoto is the center of the planning method based on *tatami* size. In buildings based on the *tatami* module it often happens that the interpost spans vary, but the second basic planning system is quite different in that it is based on the distance between the center of one post and the center of the post adjacent to it (Fig. 110). This distance is called one *ken*, which is usually roughly two meters. Although in this system the length of the *ken* is fixed, *tatami* sizes may vary.

Edo (modern Tokyo) was the center of the region employing this method.

In general, *minka* in western Japan use the *tatami* planning system (Fig. 103) and those in eastern Japan the planning system based on the interpost span (Fig. 104). The imaginary geographical line dividing these two regions runs from the Japan Alps to Mikawa Bay. Although this line served as a cultural dividing line as early as the Jomon period, posts and *tatami* were not then involved. *Tatami* existed in fairly ancient times and were used in the *shinden*-style mansions of the Kamakura period, but it was only much later that they found their way into the *minka*. It is true that *tatami* were used in the Rin'ami *minka*, built in 1397, but at that time they were considered more as furnishings on which to sit than as covering for expanses of floor of any size. It was not until after the fifteenth or the sixteenth century that the *tatami* became a *minka* flooring

113. Front view of Narai house, nineteenth century, Narakawa Village, Nagano Prefecture.

material. The mention in a pictorial record called the *Tennojiya Kaiki* of *tatami* on the floors of both the teahouse and the main *shoin*-style room of the Tennojiya in Sakai, the port for Osaka, clearly indicates that in the sixteenth century town houses of the Kinki district used these mats as flooring. It is impossible, however, to imagine that they were employed to cover floors in *minka* before the sixteenth century.

Although, as I have said, planning based on *tatami* was in general characteristic of western Japan while planning based on interpost spans was similarly characteristic of eastern Japan, three factors gave rise to a number of exceptions to this distribution pattern. First of all, political conditions resulting from the incorporation of distant areas into the administrative zone of far-removed feudal clans had an effect on planning. For example, the town houses of Kiso Fukushima, in Nagano Prefecture, employ *tatami* modules even though Nagano is actually in the part of the country where planning is usually based on interpost spans. This exception occurred because the entire Kiso valley, where Fukushima is located, belonged to the administrative—and hence cultural—sphere of Nagoya, which is in the general Kyoto cultural zone. Second, the existence of a maritime trade route between northern Honshu and western Japan resulted in the building of a few examples of *tatami*-module town houses and local landowners' homes in Yamagata, Niigata, and Akita prefectures, all of which fall geographically quite far outside the zone of Kyoto influence. Finally, to cite a reverse exception, although Kochi Prefecture, in Shikoku, falls well in the Kyoto sphere, one may find there *minka* designed on both patterns. Probably this happened because the Sekiryo Mountains served as a barrier in the transmission of the pure Kyoto style. By contrast, along

114. *Main shop of Wachusan, a firm dealing in Chinese medicines, seventeenth century, Ritto, Shiga Prefecture. (See also Figure 91.)*

the shores of the Seto Inland Sea, the *tatami*-based plan held complete sway.

As one might expect from the nature of compartmentalized feudal society, there are regional differences in the size of *tatami* themselves (Fig. 109). The differences in size reflect the differences among the clans controlling the various regions. In Kyoto the standard *tatami* is 6.3 by 3.15 *shaku* (one *shaku* equals 30.3 centimeters). Sizes in neighboring areas run somewhat smaller, and in some parts of western Japan two standard sizes exist side by side.

Like the sizes of *tatami*, the length of the standard interpost span on which the other major planning system is based varies with region and historical period. The Edo *ma*, the length assigned one *ken* or bay, was six *shaku* (slightly less than two meters). It was the most widely used standard, although some slightly larger ones existed. Research on the various

lengths of this standard is not complete, but it seems that the greatest variety occurred in the northeastern part of the country: the Tohoku region. In this zone, at the close of the Edo period, variations were quite common, just as variations in *tatami* size had been common in the Kinki district during the Muromachi period.

It is especially interesting to note how clearly the usage patterns of the above-noted floor-plan systems reflect the two large cultural spheres of Edo-period Japan. The line between the Japan Alps and Mikawa Bay was the general demarcation line between eastern and western culture. The opening of maritime trade routes between east and west did something to infuse Kyoto culture into the *minka* of eastern Japan, and this tendency increased considerably after the Meiji Restoration of 1868. With the relaxing of many of the rules of feudal govern-

115. *Oil lamps used to produce soot for making ink sticks, Kobaien, Nara City, Nara Prefecture. (See also Figure 112.)*

ment in the wake of this extremely important political event, carpenters began to travel fairly far from home, and the men from the Kyoto area naturally took their building traditions with them. Thus the number of *minka* planned on the basis of the *tatami* increased in areas formerly served mainly by designers who followed the interpost-span system.

MARKING STRUCTURAL
MEMBERS

The markings called *banzuke* are a code to indicate where posts, beams, crossbeams, braces, and other main structural members go in the total floor plan. Although the marks are used on the struts in the truss system as well, their most important application is to the posts. In the early stages of the development of the system, marks were made in black ink with a brush carried in a small holder designed to contain both brush and ink. Later, however, this proved cumbersome, and carpenters found it more convenient to crush one end of a bamboo spatula into a mass of fibers, dip it in ink, and use it to make marks. One of the oldest known examples of the use of *banzuke* markings is found in the reconstructed three-story pagoda (1711–15) at the temple Ichijo-ji in Hyogo Prefecture. The marks, of course, were not discovered until repairs had to be made on the pagoda. Similarly, since the marks do not come to light until the building is at least partly dismantled, research concerning the use of *banzuke* in *minka* is only slightly advanced, but it seems that the shift from a true writing brush to the crushed-bamboo spatula was made after the middle of the Edo period.

The systems of marking are not actually very old, having come into being in the sixteenth century.

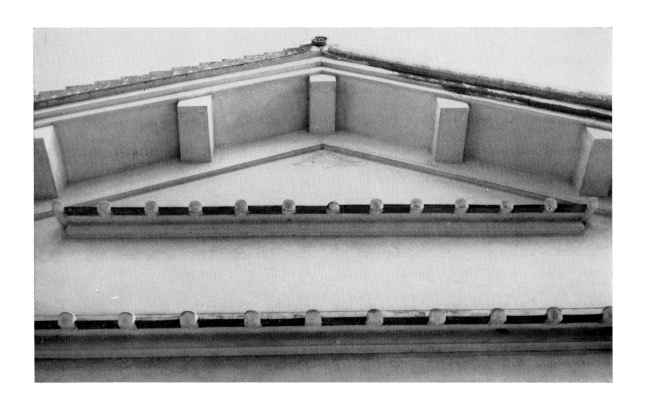

The oldest known example is found at the Kaisando of the Gyokuho-in temple, built in 1538. With the building of the great castles of the Momoyama period (1568–1603), the *banzuke* system came into general use. The oldest example of its use in a *minka* is found at the previously noted Imanishi house, built in Nara Prefecture in 1650, or only slightly after the system came to be widely applied in the residences of the great lords.

There are four main classifications of *banzuke* marks. The first, called *aimon*, or matching patterns, employs such symbols as crescents, drum shapes, and triangles. As long as the symbols remain small in number, the system works smoothly, but it becomes awkward as the number increases. It was successfully used to indicate the structural members of each story of the Hikone Castle when that edifice was rebuilt. Although no example of its use in the *minka* is known, the fact that the carpenters of the

Kiso valley region in Nagano Prefecture persist today in referring to all *banzuke* markings as *aimon* suggests that it may have been used in *minka* at one time.

The second system, the *mawari banzuke*, is a rotating system. Using either symbols of the Japanese *hiragana* syllabary or Japanese numerals, it always begins with one of the corner posts and moves around the building and inward in a clockwise spiral. Similarly, the third system, known as the *jiko banzuke*, or spiraling-incense system, is a rotating one, but only one kind of symbol is used. The name derives from a resemblance to the curling lines of incense used in Buddhist ceremonies. Of the four systems, these two are the oldest.

The fourth system, the *kumiawase*, was first developed in the Momoyama period. Employing geometrical coordinates, it indicates horizontal position with syllabary symbols and vertical posi-

116. Tile projections (mizukiri-gawara) *designed to throw off driving rains and protect clay walls, nineteenth century, Aki, Kochi Prefecture.*

117. *Roofing of miscanthus (left) and ordinary reed (right). Fukushima Prefecture.*

tion with numerals, although sometimes only one or the other serves its purpose. The *kumiawase* system is the one most widely used today.

The *mawari banzuke* and the *kumiawase banzuke* are found most often in *minka,* and they manifest a certain regional distribution. Unfortunately, however, research on this subject is insufficiently developed to make a general clarification of the picture possible. Still, one can say for certain that the eastern seaboard and the Kinki district favored the *kumiawase,* whereas the Chugoku region (western Honshu) and the island of Shikoku generally employed the *mawari banzuke.* Even in these instances, though, the lines of demarcation are inconsistent, and after the Meiji Restoration the *kumiawase* system of the Kyoto-Osaka district made serious inroads in the areas favoring the *mawari* system.

I have discussed the marking systems at some length because they are closely related to the regional distribution of the various groups of carpenters who remained more or less within their native districts as a result of the strong local ties fostered under a feudal government. The master carpenter made the markings, which were for the sole purpose of preparing the structural members, already cut, for erection at the building site. None of the markings have anything to do with the owner of the house or his wishes, and all of them are completely concealed once the building is finished. Moreover, since master carpenters passed their marking systems on to their apprentices and underlings and since technical exchange was at a minimum during the feudal period, the nature of the markings tells something about groups of carpenters and whatever relations existed among them. Regrettably, there is no other information available on this subject. Oddly enough, although intense

commercial relationships existed in the Kinki, Chugoku, and Shikoku districts, judging from the known distributions of marking systems, we can assume that technical exchange among carpenters must have been strictly suppressed.

REGIONAL STATUS   Because it evolved against
SYMBOLS   the background of Japa-
                    nese feudal society, the
minka is inevitably characterized by regional color and by traits peculiar to the feudal social structure. Generally speaking, in all ages of its development, the *minka* has been marked by regional characteristics because building techniques and planning ideas were transmitted largely from person to person, construction was carried out by manual labor, techniques were closely confined to given regions, and materials were by and large limited to those abundant in the area in which the given house was built. Among such materials, bamboo, for ex-

ample, was widely used in southern Kyushu, where it grows in profusion. Eaves of main building sections, roofs of smaller ones, floors of living areas, doors, and certain lighting fixtures were all made of bamboo. The *Saiyuzakki,* an eighteenth-century record of travels in western Japan, makes it clear that bamboo roofs and doors were typical of the *minka* of southern Kyushu. Such heavy reliance on this material is unknown in other parts of the country. Again, in regions where miscanthus rushes are difficult to obtain, shingles were used as roofing. In volcanic zones, where clay is scarce, walls were finished with either rushes or boards. There are many other examples of local traits dependent upon the availability of materials and similar factors.

One of the most notable instances of characteristic traits resulting solely from considerations of social standing is the famous L-shaped *minka* style known as *chumon-zukuri* and developed in Niigata Prefecture (Figs. 72, 118, 119). Today the *chumon-*

zukuri is considered the outstanding trait of *minka* in this part of the country, but it has not always been so, as one can learn from a remark in an old book called *Echigo Fudoko*. It was not until the Kambun era (1661–73), this work says, that the houses of villagers employed the L-shaped plan, in which a main section is joined to living quarters, kitchen, and stable. Before that time, people of the lower classes built one main building for living and accommodated other functions in outbuildings. This comment makes it clear that the *chumon-zukuri* was not used in *minka* in Niigata until well after the middle of the seventeenth century, although this is not to say that the style itself did not exist before that time. Quite the contrary, in fact, for up to that time it had been the commonest style for the residences of samurai.

Other documents of the period reveal that in 1658 the Makino family, castle lords in Niigata, issued certain regulations concerning building styles for all their retainers. These regulations stipulated that the houses of all people ranging from a managerial level and the level of samurai with a yearly stipend of more than 500 *koku* (about 2,500 bushels) of rice down to the level of lower-class warriors and retainers must all have roofs of miscanthus and had no need for the *chumon* style with its L-shaped structure or for outbuildings for storage. These provisos suggest that at the beginning of the Edo period many samurai in the domains of the Nagaoka clan, which controlled the region, had houses built in the *chumon* style.

As time passed, however, laws limiting the use of this style came to be directed more at the rural farming population than at the samurai. This turn of events indicates that the *chumon-zukuri* must have gained wide popularity outside the warrior class. In 1740, the Murayama clan issued an edict to the effect that all farmers' houses must use posts of no greater length than one *jo,* four *shaku* (about 4.24

120. Umanori *ridge ornaments on a Tamugimata-style* minka, *nineteenth century, Tamugimata, Asahi Village, Yamagata Prefecture.*

meters), that the roof must be thatched with straw, that the ceilings must be of the slatted type, that the floors must be of pounded earth, and finally that neither the L-shaped *chumon-zukuri* plan nor outbuildings for storage were necessary. Clans throughout Niigata, Yamagata, and Akita prefectures put forth numerous sumptuary edicts of this kind after the middle of the Edo period.

In summary, then, the *chumon-zukuri*, a status symbol of warrior-class residences before the second half of the seventeenth century, gradually became common for the houses of villagers and finally reached the stage at which it became a noted local characteristic of *minka* throughout northwestern Japan. Still, as an examination of existing buildings in the style will show, the *chumon-zukuri* was not used for the houses of farmers below a certain social level. That is to say, instead of penetrating the entire *minka* genre, the *chumon-zukuri*, in keeping with the rural and village social structure, became

a local characteristic of the homes of only a certain class of farmers: those who owned their own land.

A similar consideration governs the various ridge styles and ridge ornaments found in *minka*. It is not surprising that ethnical scholars, in the earlier stages of research on these houses, were first struck by ridge and ridge-ornament styles, since regional differences among these two features are strongly marked and since both are immediately conspicuous elements in the house design. A perusal of almost any book on the subject will inform one that bundles of miscanthus reeds, called *harioi* or *hari-osae*, and cross-shaped wooden members (*umanori* or *karasu*) used on ridgepoles are among the most striking of regional *minka* characteristics. In addition, the number of such rooftop elements served to indicate the owner's social status within his village. *Harioi* have the practical function of preventing rain from dripping down the ropes (or wires, as is now more often the case) that stiffen the ridge (Fig. 70).

121. Suzume-odori *(sparrow-dance) ridge ornament, Horiuchi house, eighteenth century, Shiojiri, Nagano Prefecture. (See also Figures 20, 100, 108.)*

Umanori, on the other hand, serve virtually no practical purpose, acting mainly as status symbols and ornaments (Fig. 120). Again, although the *harioi* bundles of miscanthus reeds have both functional and symbolic importance, the form of the ridge itself generally serves the symbolic purpose at the sacrifice of the functional one. For example, in the Yoshino district of Nara Prefecture there is a roofing and ridge style called the *kujiya-buki* (official's roof). Today this type of roof is considered no different from that with ordinary straw thatching, but in the past it was found only on the houses of farmers who held a certain official status. To be sure, if people of this social level had predominated in the region, the roofing style might have been merely a local characteristic, but in fact, since the number of such people was small, the *kujiya-buki* is more accurately described as a status symbol. The standing of members of the class entitled to use this kind of roof is clear from the fact that only members

of that class could become officials of a local shrine and that only a member of the group could succeed to any position generally limited to his group. Obviously, the symbolic meaning of the roof style was great. Today we do not know what the roof style for houses of the nonofficial rural class was, but, unless it had been different from the one used by officials, it would have been unnecessary to coin the phrase "official's roof style." We do know that during the Momoyama and Edo periods the style lost its significance as a symbol of the official class and came to be used for the houses of most farmers who worked their own land. Thus it was transformed into a regional characteristic of *minka* in the Yoshino district. Concurrent with this trend, the farmers of the area gradually forgot the term "official's roof style."

The *udatsu,* or extended wall (Fig. 127), is still another example of a building element that, although today it is considered primarily practical in

122. Momoyama-period row houses with udatsu: *drawing of detail from* Rakuchu Rakugai *(In and Around Kyoto) screen painted by Kano Eitoku about 1574 and now in the Uesugi Collection, Yonezawa, Yamagata Prefecture.*

its role, probably partakes more strongly of symbolism. Found today in town houses, where it serves the purpose of preventing fire, the *udatsu* did not acquire this role until the late seventeenth century at the earliest. The painted screens of the Momoyama period show houses built with such walls, which resemble coping in masonry architecture. Now, it is certainly true that if the house has a tile roof and if a miniature tile roof tops the *udatsu*, fire prevention can easily be assumed to be the *udatsu's* primary role. In fact, however, the overwhelming majority of the houses pictured on the Momoyama screens are roofed with boards, and most of the *udatsu* are topped with still more highly inflammable straw thatch. To assert that such tinderlike material is a kind of fireproofing is to strain credulity. The screens also show representations of row houses with *udatsu* that are less walls built as parts of the houses than indications of the boundaries between the individual dwellings (Fig. 122). Furthermore, in one instance, straw-thatched *udatsu* adorn the top of a plank-roofed row house while, in another, plank-topped *udatsu* serve the same function for a wooden-shingle roof. Similar *udatsu* are to be found in an early Edo-period work called the *Ozoraoboe*. In this case, however, the walls are richly

ornamented to act as symbols of status, as indications of the trustworthiness of the shops housed under the roofs, or as advertising. The mere service of indicating boundary lines between individual homes has clearly been surpassed.

I believe that the patently symbolic nature of *udatsu* as used to delineate one house from another in the row dwellings of Muromachi-period Kyoto probably developed along the following lines. At the outset, individual families rented sections of rooms in one long tenement, but later, as the people became more financially independent, they began to want to demonstrate that they were sufficiently well off to have separate homes. To symbolize this affluence, they began to use the *udatsu* to demarcate their own part of the row house from those of their neighbors. To fulfill this function, it did not matter that the *udatsu* itself was made of inflammable materials. This attitude may well be the origin of the use of the phrase "putting up an *udatsu*" to mean that one is making his way in the world. I can substantiate my theory by pointing to the obviously greater affluence of the houses topped with *udatsu* shown in the Momoyama-period screens mentioned above. I do not mean to imply, however, that the symbolizing of status was the sole purpose of Muro-

123. Shoin *window alcove, Yoshimura house, seventeenth century, Habikino, Osaka Prefecture. (See also Figures 15, 22, 39, 48, 107.)*

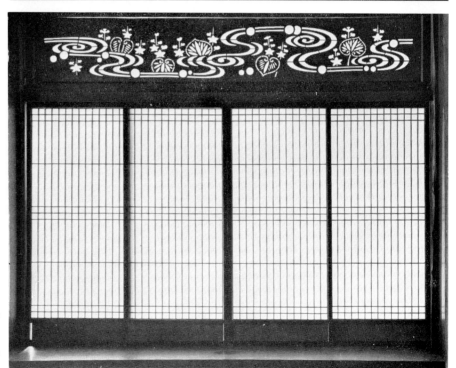

124. Shoin *window alcove, Ozaki house, eighteenth century, Hawai, Tottori Prefecture. (See also Figures 85, 90.)*

125. Stones used to hold shingles in place, Obanazawa, Yamagata Prefecture.

126. Gable-end opening and ridge ornaments on a Nosè-style minka, eighteenth century, minka village, Toyonaka, Osaka Prefecture.

machi-period *udatsu*. I definitely believe that they had a practical function and that this function came about in the fashion I shall now describe.

Generally speaking, in the houses of Kyoto from the late Heian period into Muromachi times, roofing consisted of thin wooden shingles cut from logs. Stones were placed on top of a bamboo framework on the roof to keep the shingles from flying away in the wind. This method resulted in seriously weakened eave edges and verges, which, as is often noted in documents of the time, had an alarming tendency to bend upward in a high wind. The modern *minka* solves the problem by having long strips of wood nailed on the verges and the edges of the eaves, but in premodern times, since there were no ripsaws, it was virtually impossible to obtain long pieces of

timber suited to this purpose except in the cases of powerful temples and shrines and the residences of the aristocracy. It seems likely that the builders of ordinary houses, in order to provide the necessary protection, lengthened the posts standing on the beams in the gable ends of the structure to a height that permitted the erection of a kind of coping wall rising above the roof at the verges and thus sheltering the roofing from high winds. These copings might well explain the functional origin of the *udatsu*, which later came to serve mainly a symbolic purpose.

As an interesting sidelight, I might mention that in some few cases the copinglike walls were not limited to the gable-end verges but surrounded the entire roof. Judging from the houses pictured on

127. Udatsu *(projecting wall)*, *Hasegawa house, nineteenth century, Matsuzaka, Mie Prefecture.*

128. Segaι *eaves structure, Chiba house, nineteenth century (1830), Ayaori, Tono, Iwate Prefecture. (See also Figure 66.)*

both the Machida and the Uesugi *Rakuchu Rakugai* screens, I have concluded that the eaves *udatsu* contained drains to carry away rainwater.

THE STRENGTH AND WEAKNESS OF SUMPTUARY EDICTS

The Tokugawa government, which ruled Japan from the early seventeenth until the mid-nineteenth century, was impelled on numerous occasions to issue sumptuary laws limiting the populace's expenditures on what were considered luxuries and sometimes on things that were not entirely luxurious. All of the limitations were graded according to social status. A feudal lord was obviously permitted to indulge his tastes to a much greater extent than a lowly retainer, but the gradations were much more subtle than this, extending even to distinctions among kinds of farmers. I have already shown something of this in discussing the restrictions imposed on varieties and numbers of ridge ornaments permitted to several social classes. These restrictions involved many other architectural elements, but oddly enough they were not enforced equally throughout the country. Furthermore, there was considerable difference between the strictness of the edicts imposed by the Tokugawa shogunate upon regions directly under its control and that of edicts for regions it dominated somewhat less firmly. For example, although all feudal-period clans limited the use of the tokonoma (decorative alcove) and an eaves-ceiling structure known as the *segai* (Figs. 81, 128) to certain social levels, in Kyoto, Osaka, Nara, Sakai, and other areas of the Kinki district, which were under strong Tokugawa dominance, these limitations were not in force. Generally, the tokonoma was a feature of the houses of those entitled by birth to have it or, in some cases, of the houses of rich commoners who purchased the right to construct it from the clans in whose areas they lived. But it is obvious that *minka* dwellers before the late seventeenth century had been adorning their most important rooms with this emblem of elegance, since around that time clan rulers saw fit to impose sumptuary edicts against the practice. In the Kinki district, on the other hand, as books and records as early as the Muromachi period reveal, the tokonoma and its usual companion piece the *chigai-dana,* or ornamental shelves, were to be found in *minka,* even if in less grand and decorated form than in the mansions and palaces of the great. Moreover, this custom clearly persisted into the Edo period, for one may read, in the works of the great Edo-period novelist Saikaku, of town houses with alcoves and shelves.

The previously noted Imanishi house in Nara Prefecture had no fewer than three rooms with these elegant appurtenances. All of this seems to indicate a policy of appeasement on the part of the Tokugawa shogunate toward certain of the country's older and more prestigious regions.

The case was very similar with the *segai* eaves structure, which I have mentioned above. The *segai* consists of brackets projecting outward from the tops of peripheral posts and bearing purlins to which are nailed planks connected to the main beams to form an ornamental ceiling under the eaves. In many parts of the country the *segai,* like the tokonoma, was originally confined to use in the houses of those who held some official position in town or village. Ordinary farmers were not allowed to grace their houses in this manner. Here again, however, in Kyoto, Osaka, Nara, Sakai, and their environs, inhabitants were permitted to do what was forbidden to others, since no sumptuary laws against the use of the *segai* seem to have been enforced there.

CHAPTER FOUR

Before the Minka

IN THE FIRST ICE AGE, roughly 600,000 years ago, the Japanese archipelago was part of the Asian continent, since the level of the oceans was then much lower than at present. There is no reason to believe, however, that human beings then inhabited what is now Japan. Indeed, Peking man did not appear in China until from 450,000 to 380,000 years ago, during the Second Ice Age. Japan was apparently uninhabited even then, for the first proof of human beings dwelling in this region places the date at some time during the Third Ice Age, or from 240,000 to 150,000 years ago. This proof consists of some stone implements discovered at the Fuji-san remains site in modern Gumma Prefecture.

The Japanese paleolithic period began in the latter half of the Fourth Ice Age (50,000 to 10,000 years ago), when Japan was still part of the continent and when its inhabitants relied on stones and sturdy teeth for tools. It is not surprising that mighty jaws and prominent foreheads characterized the visages of these ancient creatures. But at last, about 20,000 years ago, these people invented the stone blade, thus liberating their teeth from many doubtless troublesome chores. It is from this period that the first bones of a truly *Homo sapiens* type appear, and it was these people who developed a culture in which bones were used as a material. After another 10,000 years had passed, the inhabitants of Japan invented a stone microblade as one of their everyday accessories.

The first examples of dwellings in Japan date

from this Stone Age. One such dwelling is the sandstone Fukui Cave in Yoshii, Kita Matsuura County, Nagasaki Prefecture. Another is the Hijiridake Cave, a coal cave, at Honjo Village in Oita Prefecture. The latter, which is roughly forty meters deep, is thought to have been used for burials or for some other kind of rite. Cave dwellings from the paleolithic age are found all over the world, but during that same time, in China, some human beings still lived entirely out of doors. It may well be that, since Japan was then part of the mainland, her inhabitants too lacked even caves in which to hide their heads.

The Japanese neolithic age dawns with the closing of the Last Ice Age (10,000 to 9,000 years ago), when the first traces of the culture called the Jomon appeared. Jomon culture is named for the rope pattern (*jomon*) with which its characteristic pottery is ornamented. As the last of the great icecaps melted, bringing warmer weather and new life to the earth's vegetation, the level of the oceans rose, separating what is now Japan from the mainland and thus giving birth to the Japanese islands. The people of those times practiced no agriculture, but the abundance of pottery in their culture indicates that foraging for vegetable foods that required cooking was a more important part of their way of life than hunting. According to an estimate made by the scholar Chosuke Serizawa, during this phase of its development the Japanese population grew from a previous 2,000 to about 120,000. As the

130. *Drawing of clay* haniwa *house with* katsuogi *ridge ornaments, fifth century; found at Chausuyama tumulus, Gumma Prefecture.*

129. Minka *in Takahata, Yamagata Prefecture.*

climate became more moderate, the people added to their former cave homes, developing also a type of dwelling known as the *iwakage jukyo* (literally, "dwelling in the shadow of boulders"). Examples of cave dwellings from this age may be found at Kosegasawa in Niigata Prefecture, Hinata and Ichinosawa in Yamagata Prefecture, and Nitori in Nagano Prefecture. An example of the *iwakage jukyo* is the one at Hashidate in Saitama Prefecture.

Perhaps more important to this discussion is the appearance during the neolithic age, or Jomon period, of pit dwellings, classic examples of which are located at the Hanawadai shell mound in Ibaraki Prefecture. Among the five pit dwellings (in Japanese, *tateana jukyo*) discovered at this site, the post holes in two are irregularly situated, but the remaining three, largely similar in plan, are rectangular—about 4.9 by 3.8 meters in area (Fig. 131). The pit itself is roughly 20 centimeters deep, and there are four inner and twelve peripheral post holes. No one has been able to surmise the structure of these pit houses, but it seems likely that they were different from the ones common in later centuries. One of the most distinctive features of the group at Hanawadai is the location of the hearth outside the house in a place where it probably served as a communal facility for five families. These families may have composed one group that was constantly on the move in search of food. In any case, the fact that the hearth was outside and not inside suggests that for these people, as for all people, whether primitive or advanced, the primary purpose of the house was that of providing a place to sleep.

Toward the end of the early phase of the Jomon period, about 1,000 years later than the pit dwellings at the Hanawadai shell mound, appear the first examples of pit dwellings with indoor hearths. The remains of one such house are located at the Kode shell mound in Chiba Prefecture (Fig. 132). The plan of the house is a rectangle roughly five by three meters with a pit about thirty centimeters deep. There are two post holes in the center of the area and thirty-eight holes around the periphery. The depths of the peripheral post holes vary.

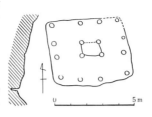

131 (top left). *Plan of pit dwelling without indoor hearth, Jomon period, Hanawadai shell mound, Ibaraki Prefecture.*

132 (top right). *Plan of pit dwelling with indoor hearth, Jomon period, Kode shell mound, Chiba Prefecture.*

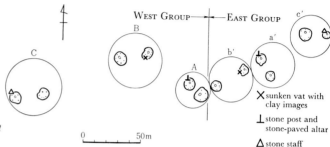

133. *Plan of Jomon-period pit-dwelling settlement at Yosukeone, Nagano Prefecture.*

During this stage of its development the pit dwelling shows certain regional differences. Although the rectangular plan is common among those found in the Kanto district (the area of which Tokyo is the center), circular plans are predominant in the Chubu district (the area of central Honshu running from Niigata Prefecture in the north to Shizuoka and Aichi prefectures in the south), Kyushu, and the northeastern part of Honshu (the Tohoku district). It seems likely that the differences in plan indicate structural differences as well, but insufficient data prohibits further speculation on the causes of these local characteristics.

In the latter half of the early Jomon period (about 3100 B.C.) extensive settlements of pit dwellings developed, usually around communal plaza-like open areas. The Minamibori shell mound in Yokohama, a good example of such settlements, consists of a group of pit dwellings arranged in a horseshoe on top of a flat elevation about thirty by fifty meters in area. It is thought that there was once a spring near the central court. A similar though much larger settlement (one hundred by two hundred meters) was discovered at the site of the Togariishi remains in Nagano Prefecture. This settlement also centered on an open plaza. The dwellings at this site are either round or rounded rectangles in plan and have diameters ranging from four to five meters. The stone-surrounded hearths are either in the centers or at the northern ends of the dwellings. A skirting wall, about thirty-five centimeters high, encloses each dwelling, and beyond it is a peripheral trough dug in the ground.

The pit-dwelling settlement found north of Togariishi at Yosukeone is especially interesting because, according to research by Masayoshi Mizuno (*History of Japan*, volume 1), its houses were divided into two large groups consisting of three distinct types (Fig. 133). The first type was ornamented with a stone post at the innermost wall or on the left side of the house. In front of this was a stone-paved altar. In the second type, at either the right or the left inside the entrance, were found sunken jugs or vats containing clay images. Each vat was surrounded by a row of stones. In the third type a stone staff was placed at either the right or the left inside the entrance. The significance of the three kinds of differentiation lies in their suggestion of some kind of functional variation within one pit-dwelling form. In addition, it seems that certain seating arrangements were used to indicate status within the family. Shamanistic practices and especially the use of the clay images called *dogu* became very common in the middle Jomon period (3000–2000 B.C.), and in the late Jomon period (2000–200 B.C.) large pit dwellings equipped with numerous ritualistic objects came into use. The remains found at Shimpukuji in Saitama Prefecture illustrate this development, for the pit dwelling there is more than ten meters to a side. From this it is clear that pit dwellings connected with magic rites came to be considered as functionally altogether different from ordinary pit dwellings. Although it is impossible to know whether this separation of function has any relationship with the shrine architecture of the succeeding Yayoi period (200 B.C. to A.D. 250), the very separation itself and the emergence of primitive religious functions are the most striking characteristics of this age.

With the beginning of the Yayoi period and the concomitant dawning of Japanese agricultural civilization, the pit dwelling enters a new phase of technical development. Because the people of the paleolithic and neolithic ages possessed no sophisticated tools, they could not achieve effective architectural joining of any kind, and they relied on ropes or vines to bind the members of a structure together. With the arrival of the Yayoi period, however, and with the iron tools known to the people of that age, it became possible to prepare proper tenons and mortises. The importance of this technical advance goes far beyond the convenience of mortised joints, for it made possible new kinds of buildings with different characteristics and buildings of much larger size than could previously be erected. The storehouses, elevated houses, and ground-level houses that appear during the Yayoi age could never have been built without the use of iron tools. Since these tools were used more for the construction of shrines and elevated storehouses than for that of dwellings, it is apparent that the buildings designed to house magical rites and ceremonies—already distinguished in a primitive fashion in the Jomon period—achieved complete architectural distinction and special exterior forms in the Yayoi period. Moreover, although the pit dwellings of the two ages resemble each other superficially, new joining methods probably brought about considerable alterations in the later buildings.

The classic examples of Yayoi-period pit dwellings are to be seen at the restored Toro remains in Shizuoka Prefecture (Figs. 134–37). This settlement probably consisted of at least twenty buildings, each oval in plan, ranging from 5.1 to 7.1 meters in the long axis and from 4.5 to 6 meters in the short axis and surrounded by a low plank wall about 30 centimeters in height. At the base of each of the four main sunken posts was attached a foundation board. The restoration on view to the public today was planned by Professor Masaru Sekino.

Extant records indicate that the pit dwelling persisted into the late sixteenth or the early seventeenth century, but more dramatic was the discovery of two such houses when a river bank in Akita Prefecture collapsed as a result of a flood in 1861. These houses are thought to have been buried in a flood that occurred during the Keicho era (1596–1615). Neither house was very large, but one had several interesting features (Fig. 148). Its pit was so deep that a stepladder was required to reach the entrance, which was fitted with a double-leaf door made of two fairly thick boards. The posts, which were rectangular in cross section, were from 6.2 to 6.3 *shaku* (about 1.88 meters) in length, and the beams, which were trapezoidal in cross section, were from 10 to 16 *shaku* (3.03 to 4.85 meters) long.

A second important advance in the Yayoi period was the functional separation of the house and the storehouse. In earlier times grain had been kept in the pit dwelling itself, but in this age a separate elevated storehouse came into use. On a projecting piece of land among somewhat lower rice paddies at Tsuyama in Okayama Prefecture are the Numa remains, which consist of five pit dwellings sur-

134. *Remains of Yayoi-period pit dwelling at Toro, Shizuoka Prefecture.*

135. *Reconstruction of Yayoi-period pit dwelling at Toro, Shizuoka Prefecture.*

136. *Detail showing* nezumi-gaeshi *(device to prevent entry by rats) on reconstructed Yayoi-period elevated storehouse at Toro, Shizuoka Prefecture.*

137. *(right). Detail showing corner structure of reconstructed Yayoi-period elevated storehouse at Toro, Shizuoka Prefecture.*

138. Back of bronze mirror with relief showing four different house styles, third to fourth century; found at Samida tumulus, Nara Prefecture.

rounding another ruin that may have been either a working place or a storehouse. The entire settlement is semicircular and is partly surrounded by a trench. Outside the trench are five communal-use elevated storehouses. The similar storehouse reconstructed beside the pit dwellings at the above-mentioned Toro site was based on data obtained from excavations at the Yamagi remains in Nirayama, Shizuoka Prefecture.

Two interesting aspects of this building type deserve notice. First, in architectural style the elevated storehouse resembles the main building at the Grand Shrine of Ise, which for ages has preserved its traditional form through periodic rebuildings. Second, the storehouse required much more extensive use of iron tools in its construction than did the pit dwelling.

Certainly with the extensive growth of wet-rice cultivation, land development, and riparian works that took place in the Yayoi period, it is only common sense to assume that some kind of leader had to emerge to take control of operations. Un-

fortunately we have no material to suggest the influence that the evolution of a ruling class had on the form and nature of the pit dwelling. For this part of the story one must wait until the opening of the Tumulus period (250–552). The most outstanding piece of evidence for social status as reflected in domestic architecture is the third-to-fourth-century bronze mirror (Fig. 138) found at the Samida tumulus in Nara Prefecture. On the back of this mirror is a relief showing four clearly different house styles.

The first of these styles (at left in the photograph) is an elevated and gabled building with the entrance in the gable end. It is apparently either a shrine or a storehouse. Probably two bays square, the plan of the building recalls that of the main building of the Izumo Shrine. There is a long staircase leading upward at one gable end.

The second structure (top in the photograph) was possibly the home of a chieftain. It too is elevated, and the entrance is on the gable end, but its roof is of the hipped-and-gabled type. A long wooden staircase with a handrail leads to one gabled end. On the other end is an exposed platform and a long-handled parasol of the type once used by people of high rank. The parasol projects diagonally outward from the building. The building itself is three bays long in the ridge direction, and the other dimension, although it is uncertain, is probably either two or three bays.

The third building (right in the photograph), though topped with a hipped-and-gabled roof, rests on the ground. It too is three bays long in the ridge direction and probably two or three bays across the gable end.

The fourth of these buildings (bottom in the photograph) is a pit dwelling of the kind traditional since the Jomon period. Its roof extends to the ground, and there is no lower skirting wall. The projecting line on the left may be a raisable door at the entrance.

In all likelihood these four building types reflect not only functional differences but also the social strata in settlements of the times. The ancient house styles could scarcely differ more from the *minka* as it is known today, but it would not do to overlook some striking similarities. First, the incline of the gables in the ancient dwellings is sharply upward and to the front. Second, the bargeboards in both cases project beyond the roof, and the rafters in the ancient houses also project beyond the ridge to form *chigi*, an architectural feature similar to the *umanori* ridge ornaments that I have previously discussed.

Another house similar in these respects to both the *minka* and the ancient houses seen on the mirror back is charmingly represented in the clay *haniwa* houses (Fig. 130). *Haniwa*, the clay figures of human beings, animals, houses, and the like made to ornament the great grave mounds, or tumuli, from which the age derives its name, were produced in considerable numbers from the second half of the third century until some time in the seventh century. At the Chausuyama tumulus, in Gumma Prefecture, eight *haniwa* houses thought to date from the fifth century have been discovered. The one that seems to be the main house of the set is a gabled structure with the entrance on the side parallel with the ridge. Its plan is a rectangle three bays by two, and the ridgepole is topped by six loglike ornaments called *katsuogi* (Fig. 130). In addition to this house there are two subordinate gabled houses two bays by two with entrances on the sides parallel to the ridges and with an *ajiro* (woven split bamboo) cover over the ridge in place of the *katsuogi*. Three elevated storehouses two bays by two with entrances on the sides parallel to the ridges, another elevated storehouse with a similar entrance but with a hipped roof, and one ground-level shedlike building with a gabled roof and an entrance on the side parallel to the ridge complete the set, except for a clay object that seems to represent a plank fence. Functional differentiation is quite clearly marked in all of these *haniwa* buildings.

As the social distinctions symbolized by these functional differences intensified, palaces and mansions of the aristocrats came into existence. These residences are closely related to Asian continental styles and techniques and therefore are fundamentally apart from the *minka* tradition. Mansions first developed during the Tumulus period. Both the *Kojiki* and the *Nihon Shoki*, Japan's oldest historical records, contain clear indications that the residence of the emperor had become an important symbol of dignity and rank by the time of the emperor Yuryaku—that is, the second half of the fifth century. For one thing, these chronicles tell us that the emperor ordered one Shiki no O-ogatanushi to remove from the ridgepole of his house the *katsuogi*, which were by then regarded as a symbol of imperial authority and were consequently forbidden to all but the emperor. Second, we learn that a certain Manè, grandson of an immigrant master carpenter, began to build a "towered palace" for the emperor at this time.

From this age on, the *minka* and the residences of the nobility followed two separate paths of development. Unlike the mansions of the noble and the rich, the *minka* has left hardly any traces of its development from this period until the sixteenth century. There are neither materials for direct research into the matter nor remains of any significance. The sole sources of information are the pictures and the regional records.

CHAPTER FIVE

The Minka from Medieval to Early Modern Times

FOR VERY EARLY stages in the development of the *minka*, one may turn to fairly numerous remains of the kinds I have already discussed, but for the period from then until the early eighteenth century directly related material of any comprehensive nature does not exist. Of course there are the two remaining *sennenya*, or thousand-year houses, and others like the Kuriyama house (1607) in Gojo in Nara Prefecture (Figs. 94, 152), the Imanishi house (1650) in Kashihara in Nara Prefecture (Figs. 5, 40, 46, 67, 74), and the Takemura house (1684) in Komagane in Nagano Prefecture (Fig. 7), but their number is very small, and all of them have undergone such extensive renovation and alteration that it is extremely difficult to know what they looked like when they were first built. In addition, quite by accident, most of the remaining houses have certain traits that make it dubious that they were built in the general style of their times. There are other houses that may be of considerable age, but because of the lack of any evidence—for example, the ceremonial ornament dated and attached to the ridge when the framework was completed or ink inscriptions stating the year of construction—most of these are unreliable material.

In order to make some attempt at filling the gap between the very ancient and the much more recent *minka*, I must resort to secondary sources.

Even these will not give a systematic history of *minka* development, but they may provide some enlightening glimpses.

HOUSES OF THE HEIAN & KAMAKURA PERIODS

Literary works of the Heian and Kamakura periods mention a style of house known as the *tsuboya*, or "jar house." The name of this style, apparently used for houses with special functions rather than for general residences, derives from the fact that the entrance was the only opening in the small building, for there were no windows. These dark little houses were often the abodes of poor women, servants, nuns, and others of humble calling, and when they were the true residences of such persons they fell into the middle or low social bracket. In addition, they sometimes served as places of retirement for elderly people who had renounced the world for a life of solitude, or they were used as storage sheds. One may find ancient texts that mention, for example, a pair of brothers who engaged in hunting deer and wild boar and had a *tsuboya* in which their retired mother lived. We also learn from such texts that a certain high-ranking prelate named Kanken Shonin stored palanquins in a *tsuboya* and that at the mansion of the lord of Yamato *tsuboya* served as sleeping quarters for the samurai.

139. Detail from twelfth-century Nenju Gyoji *picture scroll showing Kyoto shop-residence of late Heian period.*

140. Detail from twelfth-century Shigi-san Engi *picture scroll showing late-Heian-period home of the rich man Yamazaki.*

141. Detail from fourteenth-century Kasuga Gongen Reigen Ki *picture scroll showing Kamakura-period clay storehouse.*

142. Detail from fourteenth-century Matsuzaki Tenjin Engi *picture scroll showing Kamakura-period home of a poor copper worker.*

In the famous scroll paintings (*emaki*) of the Heian and Kamakura periods we see many town houses and a few rural *minka*. The characteristics of the town houses of these periods, as they appear in the scrolls, include board roofs and board walls or sometimes walls of woven split bamboo (*ajiro*) or clay, high-placed windows fitted with upward-swinging shutters called *hajitomi*, and main entrances with inward-swinging wooden doors. All of the houses pictured in these scrolls must be to some extent taken with a grain of salt, for they frequently represent less of realism than of the imagination of the artist. Moreover, artists sometimes portrayed *minka* they had never seen, and more often than not the time of the production of the scroll painting and that depicted in the story the scroll tells are separated by a considerable gap. In spite of all these drawbacks, however, the picture scrolls may be regarded as showing at least some aspects of the *minka* as they existed in those distant times.

143. Detail from thirteenth-century Ippen Shonin Eden picture scroll showing Kamakura-period houses.

144. Detail from thirteenth-century Ippen Shonin Eden picture scroll showing Kamakura-period mountain farmhouse.

To elaborate a bit on the information provided by several of the most famous scrolls from the twelfth through the fourteenth century, I shall cite a few illustrations taken from them. In the fourth part of the twelfth-century *Nenju Gyoji Emaki* (Picture Scroll of Annual Rites and Ceremonies), for example, we see a shop with fish drying on an outdoor shelf. The shop walls are a combination of *ajiro* and horizontally and vertically set boards. The door swings inward, and there seems to be an earth-floored passage-entranceway (Fig. 139). In the fifth part of this same work is a picture of a board-roofed town house with *ajiro*-covered walls and with the above-noted upward-swinging *hajitomi* shutters. In the twelfth part of the scroll we see a row of buildings used in this case as a kind of reviewing stand for the famous Kyoto Hollyhock Festival. The true function of these buildings is a matter of dispute, for some scholars believe that they were actually row houses, whereas others hold that they were probably shops. At any rate, the picture shows quite clearly the structure of the gable end of the

row. Each section is three bays by two, with an earth-floored area at one side, a board-covered roof topped with what appear to be bundles of reeds, and logs to help hold the roofing in place. The walls on the long sides are covered with *ajiro*, but the gable-end wall is made of boards. The purlins are square in cross section, and there is a sliding door between the earth-floored area and the true interior.

In the "flying storehouse" section of the twelfth-century *Shigi-san Engi* (Legends of Mount Shigi) scroll there is a picture of the house of a certain rich man named Yamazaki (Fig. 140). This house probably cannot be placed in the *minka* category. Although the floor plan is of the *minka* type, the details seem to belong more to the tradition of the *shinden*-style mansions of the aristocracy. In the same scroll, however, we find a picture of a town house in Nara with *hajitomi* on the windows and walls that are a combination of vertically set boards and clay.

The thirteenth-century *Ippen Shonin Eden* (Pic-

145. *Beamwork and earth-floored area, Egawa house, eighteenth century (1707), Nirayama, Shizuoka Prefecture. (See also Figure 4.)*

torial Life of Saint Ippen) contains more pictures of *minka* than any other similar work. From among them I have selected two to illustrate the types shown. The fifth section of the scroll shows a group of town houses in Kamakura (Fig. 143). All of them have board roofs that are either gabled or hipped and gabled, board walls, shop shelves, *hajitomi*, large openings, and inward-swinging doors. In the first section of the scroll we see a representation of architecture in the region of severe winters in northern Honshu: a large *minka* with a hipped and thatched roof and a board-roofed outbuilding (Fig. 144).

In the fourteenth-century *Kasuga Gongen Reigen Ki* (Legends of the Kasuga Gongen Miracles), which deals with events centering on the celebrated Kasuga Shrine in Nara, we find an interesting "storehouse that escaped a fire" (Fig. 141). The roof is gone, but one can see that the building itself is a thoroughly fireproof structure built in a style not unlike that used in warehouses of the much later Edo period. It is also interesting to note that this is

the first known picture of a clay storehouse to appear in Japanese art.

Finally, in the fourteenth-century *Matsuzaki Tenjin Engi* (Legends of the Matsuzaki Tenjin Shrine), there appears the house of a "poor copper worker" (Fig. 142). In fact, the house is far from looking as poor as the text of the scroll states. Indeed, it is doubtful that one is safe in calling it a *minka*. The walls and the roof are made of boards. There is an open veranda in front of the house, and *tatami* appear together with wooden floors. Wood-paneled sliding doors called *mairado* are used as partitions, and there is a hearth in the middle of the floor of one room. We can also see that the entrance to the sleeping quarters resembles the *chodai*-room door structure (see pages 142–43).

The first truly reliable information available on *minka* in the middle period of their development is an early-fourteenth-century set of records from two villages, both of which today are part of the town of Toba, near Kyoto. The records contain data on 107 houses which belonged to *honzaike*, or farmers

146. *Urban houses in Muromachi-period Kyoto: detail from sixteenth-century* Raku-chu Rakugai *(In and Around Kyoto) screen, Machida Collection, Tokyo.*

of long-established position, and 135 which belonged to *shinzaike,* or newly independent farmers. The dwellings of the latter, for obvious reasons, were smaller than those of the former. The following four interesting points emerge from an examination of these records.

First, the majority of the houses had square plans. Second, the overwhelming majority had entrances in the gable end. Of the few buildings with entrances on the side parallel to the ridge, large *minka* predominate, and the largest one recorded has such an entrance. Third, most of the houses were quite small, 28 percent being less than 4 *tsubo* (13.2 square meters) in area and 82 percent being less than 12 *tsubo* (39.7 square meters). Finally, since the records show that many of the landowning farmers employed numerous tenants (*hikan hyakusho*), some of the houses listed may well have been the homes of hired laborers. The records further substantiate this supposition by stating that the homes of the tenants were scattered throughout the villages instead of being close to the homes of the landowners.

THE RIN'AMI HOUSE AND THE JITOGATA MANDOKORO

The oldest extant example of a *minka* floor plan is that of the Rin'ami house, which an influential landowning farmer outfitted with a statue of the Jizo Bodhisattva and donated to the Kyoto temple To-ji in 1397, the year in which the framework of the famous Temple of the Golden Pavilion was completed. The floor-plan drawing that is today the property of the To-ji shows the layout of the house as it was in that year (Fig. 149). As I have noted earlier, the truss structure of the Rin'ami house was probably of the *odachi* type. The house was rectangular in plan, four bays by six, and the entrance was in the gable end. Documents at the To-ji include a list of all the furnishings donated with the house. The building contained, in addition to three ordinary rooms, a small Buddhist chapel and a *chodai*-style room that was probably the sleeping quarters. There was also an earth-floored section with a cooking stove, as well as a room that was probably used for storage. The exterior walls were covered with vertically set boards. Some of

147. Urban houses in Momoyama-period Kyoto: detail from sixteenth-century Raku-chu Rakugai *(In and Around Kyoto) screen, Tokyo National Museum.*

the openings were equipped with *shitomido* shutters, and a swinging one-leaf door was hung at the entrance. It is known that there were ten *tatami* mats in the building, and in all likelihood they were placed in the room in which important guests were received. There were also sixteen *shoji*, and, like most *minka shoji* of the Muromachi period, they had bamboo instead of wooden frames.

In the possession of the To-ji and the Tokyo National Museum are copies of floor-plan layouts for a building that was called the Jitogata Mandokoro (administrative office) of the Niimi manor (located today in the city of Niimi, Okayama Prefecture) but was in fact the home of a farmer-samurai known as Nara-dono (Fig. 150). The house was moved to the Niimi manor in 1464. Although the post positions in the two extant plans differ slightly, the floor plans are quite similar. The house plan is a rectangle four bays by six and a half and closely resembles the floor plans of both the Hakogi *sennenya* and the Rin'ami house. There were two rooms for ordinary living purposes (one with an exposed veranda), a *chodai* room, and a storage room. There may not have been an earth-floored section in this house, and the kitchen, which was not part of the original structure, consisted of two buildings moved to the Niimi site from the home of a tenant farmer and joined in an L shape. The floors of the kitchen sections, both of which were rectangles five bays by three, were probably originally of pounded earth.

SENNENYA Up to this point I have referred from time to time to *sennenya*, or thousand-year houses. I shall now explain this term somewhat more fully. *Sennenya* is a name applied in Hyogo Prefecture to very old *minka*. As I have noted, the Hakogi *sennenya* had already acquired the appellation by 1790, and it seems likely that it was the first house to do so. Although it differs radically in plan and structure from the general run of *minka* of its period, records state that the style was prevalent in the mountain regions. At any rate, after the Hakogi *minka* came to be known as a *sennenya*, the name became common for all very old houses in the Hyogo region. Since there are

148. *Nineteenth-century drawing of pit dwelling thought to have been buried in a flood during the Keicho era (1596–1615); unearthed during a flood in 1861 at Yoneshirogawa, Akita Prefecture.*

legends to the effect that the *sennenya* date from as early as the Daido era (806–10), they are sometimes called Daido houses, but the probability that they are actually that old is slender indeed.

Only two *sennenya* are still extant: the Hakogi house and the Furui house (the latter in the town of Antomi, Hyogo Prefecture), but in the past there were a number of others. The Sakata *sennenya*, which was destroyed by fire in 1962, was located in Kobe. It was called the "board house" because its walls and partitions were made of boards. The wide boards, similar to modern panels, used in the largest guest room of the house suggested a possible forerunner of the Muromachi-period tokonoma. Records make it clear that this house already existed in 1568.

The Daiji *sennenya*, formerly located in Imada, Hyogo Prefecture, was destroyed by fire in 1775. Built of pine, it was a sizable house, and there is a legend to the effect that the great general Minamoto Yoshitsune sojourned there during the Gen-

ryaku era (1184–85). Two other houses of the *sennenya* type, both formerly located in Kobe, were destroyed by fire in 1628.

Although, as I have noted, there is absolutely nothing to prove that houses of the *sennenya* type date from the Daido era of the early ninth century, certainly they are at least as old as the Muromachi period, and some would claim that they can be reasonably dated as early as the Kamakura period. Still others hold that the construction styles correspond with those used in the Heian period, but this is not to imply that the *sennenya* were necessarily being built in late Heian times.

The *sennenya* suggest that many homes of farmer-samurai or influential small landholders in the Hyogo region had rectangular plans about four bays by six. Still, it is possible that in the Muromachi period the houses of members of these social classes were much larger. For instance, late-seventeenth-century records dealing with a residence in Noto, Ishikawa Prefecture, describe the kitchen, which was built in 1580, as being three bays wide and eleven bays long. Again, the kitchen of the Egawa house in Nirayama, Shizuoka Prefecture (Fig. 145), is very large. It is true that this structure was rebuilt after having been destroyed by an earthquake in 1707, but much of the original building material was used. Therefore it probably retains something very like its original appearance. Legend gives the date of the building of the main part of the house as 1483, and there seems to be good reason to accept either this date or some date not too far removed as correct. The house itself has been much repaired and enlarged, but its present size indicates that it would have had to be fairly large at the outset. It should be noted that kitchens as spacious as those I have been describing served not only for the preparation of food but also as sleeping quarters for low-ranking members of the household.

URBAN HOUSES OF 16TH-CENTURY NARA AND KYOTO

Moving on to urban *minka*, I should like first to discuss briefly the nature of this kind of residence in sixteenth-century Nara. Much information on the widths of house openings and on the relationship between house and building site is available in records dating from the Tensho era (1573–92), especially in records of contributions made to a festival held each May at the great Kasuga Shrine in Nara. This material makes it clear that urban houses of the common people were, on an average, ten or eleven *shaku* (3.03 or 3.33 meters) in width. The narrowest mentioned is 7.5 *shaku* (2.27 meters), while the widest is 18 *shaku* (5.45 meters). In addition, these records and others show that at this time a considerable amount of space separated one urban house from another. That is to say, the Nara houses did not form a continuous row as did the Kyoto houses shown on the painted screens of the times. Again, numerous measurement figures entered in one set of records reveal a great many details about the daily life of the citizens of Nara in the Muromachi period.

For instance, mention is made of a kind of duplex dwelling called the *aiya*. Not only the structure but also the word itself is today little known in Nara or elsewhere, but in the Muromachi period houses divided to serve two families were not uncommon. The division of a single house into two was usually carried out for one of two reasons. In some cases the heirs to a father's property saw fit to divide everything equally, including the house. Consequently, one finds mention of a house divided down the middle and occupied by two brothers and their families. The second reason for the split into a duplex dwelling involved financial failure. For instance, there is a sad story about a man who made his living by repairing the roofs of a local Nara shrine. He was a master worker, but when the shrine and the temple with which it was associated fell into financial difficulties he too felt the pinch. In order to make ends meet, he sold half of his house, thus limiting himself and his family to the other half.

People whose purses were better lined did not have to go to such drastic lengths. In fact, the general practice for large families was to develop a compound of small individual houses for the various units among their members. These arrangements too are described in extant records: a compound of

149. *Plan of Rin'ami house, fourteenth century (1397), in archives of the Kyoto temple To-ji.*

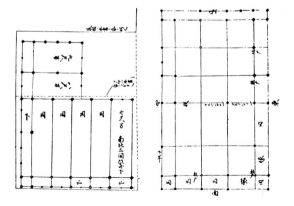

150. *Plan of Jitogata Mandokoro (Niimi Manor), fifteenth century (1464), in archives of the Kyoto temple To-ji.*

151. *Detail of Hakogi* sennenya, *probably fourteenth or fifteenth century, Yamada-cho, Hyogo-ku, Kobe. (See also Figures 1, 12.)*

152. *Smoke vent, Kuriyama house, seventeenth century* ▷ *(1607), Gojo, Nara Prefecture. (See also Figure 94.)*

four buildings for a family of nine, a single building for a single person, and the like. But the records are not entirely trustworthy, for owners, ostensibly for tax reasons, were not above admitting to fewer buildings than they actually possessed.

Before leaving this subject, I should like to make a comment about houses that can only be called "rentals" in English but whose occupancy did not involve monetary transactions. It is true that in the Edo period rentals of the generally accepted kind were the rule, but the word *kashiya*, which came to mean a house rented for money, had a different meaning in the sixteenth century. At that time a *kashiya* was the dwelling of tenants or underlings of the head of a household. No matter whether these people were related by blood to the head of the house or were simply in his employ, money was not taken from them for the use of the *kashiya*.

SCREEN PAINTINGS depicting the manners and mores of the people offer considerable information about the town houses of Kyoto during the full flowering of Momoyama-period (1568–1603) culture. At a glance the general exterior appearances of the houses pictured on the screens seem very much like those of Kyoto town houses of today, but details differ sharply between the two periods. From the Kuriyama house (1607) and the Imanishi house (1650) it is possible to tell that the interiors were considerably plainer than those of later *minka*, even though the exteriors employed the gables and gable ornaments found in castles and temples.

A room called the *chodai*, with board walls on three sides and ornamental sliding doors, is a characteristic feature of these houses. The *chodai* was used as sleeping quarters and as a storage place for valuables. Simplified versions of it appear in farmhouses of the Edo period, and, although it was formerly thought that *chodai* did not appear in early-Edo town houses, it has lately been learned that they did exist in such buildings during that period. Moreover, in picture scrolls from as early as the Kamakura period, one may find representations of town houses with *chodai* similar to the one in

of the kind and number of animals (chiefly horses and cows) they possessed. Obviously this material is a rich source of information about the *minka*. The oldest of such records, dating from 1622 and concerned with Buzen Province (modern Fukuoka Prefecture), are unsuitable, however, for research on the *minka*, and the first to be of value in this respect are those from 1633 dealing with Hizen Province (modern Saga Prefecture). This record makes it clear that the *minka* of the seventeenth century were quite different from those found in the same region today. First of all, the kitchen was placed in an outbuilding, as were the sleeping quarters of the hired hands. In some compounds, in fact, the family sitting room, the Buddhist-altar room, the stable, the family sleeping quarters, and the like were all separate structures. Three hundred years later, however, the kitchen and the main building had come together in the so-called two-ridge building style.

Another set of census records of this type, dating from 1644 and listing the numbers of houses and people in several villages in the vicinity of modern Osaka, reveals the relative smallness of *minka* of the period. The overwhelming majority, it appears, were a mere three bays by two. (One bay equals about two meters.) As one might suspect, the houses occupied by the heads of the usually extensive family groups were larger than others. The evidence for cramped quarters in the same period is strengthened by a list of people and domestic animals in a certain village in the present Mie Prefecture. The list, made in 1647, notes that the main house of a farmer who kept three men and two women workers was a rectangle no more than three by six bays—the very minimum size for modern *minka*. In addition to the main house there were two outbuildings, one of which served as sleeping quarters for the hired men. (Presumably the hired women slept in the main house.)

Certain regional differences in size appeared in *minka* of this time, as a set of records from Nagano Prefecture indicate. These records, for the town of Omachi for 1649, state that the majority of main farmers' houses were either three by five bays or four by five bays—that is, twice as large as similar

the Imanishi house. The wooden walls are made of horizontal boards supported by notched braces in the rear, and the ornamental sliding doors, which may be either single or double, move on a sill that is raised some 15 to 18 centimeters above floor level. The original purpose of the elevated sill was to prevent the scattering of straw kept in the *chodai* room for use as fuel and bedding in older times. Later, when the now common *futon* (heavy quilts) came into use as bedding, this raised doorway continued in existence as an ornamental convention. In addition, although there are cases in which the grooves for the sliding doors run the full length of the lintel and the sill, in some instances, probably because of a particular but now forgotten function, we find that the grooves stop about halfway across the opening.

HOUSES OF THE EARLY EDO PERIOD

Records of the early Edo period take account not only of the number of people and the kinds of houses they lived in but also houses in the Kinki district. The smallest houses were only one by two bays, an incredibly small size, whereas the largest (ten by eleven bays) corresponded to the size of modern basic-ridge *minka*. A similar set of documents from Nagano for 1654 reveals similar *minka* sizes and furnishes information on the nature of roofing materials and foundation stones. Roofs for main houses and dwellings for hired workers were of the usual boards or miscanthus rushes. All of the workers' dwellings and 80 percent of the main houses had posts that were partly buried in the ground without foundations of any kind. Other contemporary documents substantiate this evidence. Small houses with partly buried posts appear to have remained the predominant pattern until the beginning of the nineteenth century, when building techniques altered radically.

Finally, from the work of the nineteenth-century writer Kobayashi Kuzuko, it is possible to glean a few more interesting pieces of information. He tells us that it was usual to char the ends of posts before sinking them into the ground and that foundation stones first appeared in *minka* of the Saku area in Nagano Prefecture in the house of a certain Oribe, who died in 1657. We also learn from this source that doors of split and woven bamboo were much more common than wooden ones until the second half of the seventeenth century; that earth floors were more frequent than wooden floors until the same period; and that posts were generally finished with an adze or a type of plane called a *yariganna*.

CHAPTER SIX

Shops and Farmhouses of the Edo Period

SHOPS OF THE EDO PERIOD In the Edo period, merchants from Ise (present Mie Prefecture) and Omi (present Shiga Prefecture) established shops in the major cities—Kyoto, Osaka, and Edo. These shops were called Isedana and Omidana, names that not only signify the home provinces of the merchant families but also stand for a special kind of building. The first of the aspects that set these buildings apart from the general run of buildings is the fact that the owner and his family did not live in them but resided in either Ise or Omi. Managers, clerks, other assistants, and the son of the family who was charged with superintending the shop did live in the building, but their occupancy failed to influence the floor plan. Many buildings of the Isedana and Omidana type (or Iseya and Omiya, as they later came to be called) stood in old Edo, but for the sake of conciseness I shall describe only one of them: the Daikokuya, a famous Edo-period dry-goods enterprise with outlets in Kyoto and Osaka as well as in Edo and with a stock-acquiring facility in what is now Gumma Prefecture. The home office and shop, built in Nihombashi, Edo, during the Kyoho era (1716–36), had a frontage of six bays and a depth of more than sitxeen bays. It was two stories in height, measuring 17.5 *shaku* (5.30 meters) from ground to eaves, and had a tile roof. At the front on the first floor were twelve sliding wooden doors covered with copper that was in turn thickly coated with plaster. The second floor was furnished with compartments for its shutters. In short, the building was a combination shop and traditional clay-walled storehouse. Since this style understandably became fashionable after the great fire of the Kyoho era, the Daikokuya represented the latest thing in shops when it was first built.

The completely unpartitioned first floor was given over entirely to the shop. At the entrance was a wide, shallow earth-floored section, and the remainder of the area had a plank floor. The ceiling was high, and there were three fireproof underground storage vaults beneath the floor. The second floor consisted of storage space and sleeping quarters. In addition to the main building, the site contained a smaller shop (three by six and one-half bays), two three-story storehouses, still another storehouse, and a kitchen building three by nine bays divided into two sections, one earth-floored and one board-floored. The last-mentioned storehouse was divided into two sections, and the spacious kitchen building contained a hearth, stoves for cooking, and a bath. This was no doubt the building in which the employees of the company ate their meals.

The *Morisada Manko,* a virtual small encyclo-

153. Shihobuta-*style* minka, *eighteenth century, Aisumi, Tokushima Prefecture.*

154. Minka *with hipped and gabled roof, eighteenth century, originally in Tsuruga, Fukui Prefecture, and now in* minka *village, Toyonaka, Osaka Prefecture.*

pedia of ethnic material written by Kitamura Morisada in 1853, notes that the town houses of Kyoto and Osaka were more or less all alike, whereas those of Edo were more varied. I am afraid this comment is often misunderstood today. What Kitamura intended to say was that in Kyoto all of the town houses featured a long earth-floored passage (*toriniwa*) that ran from the front to the back of the house and were in this sense similar. In contrast, the Edo town houses followed highly fragmented and therefore never uniform plans of the kind represented by the Daikokuya. The floor-plan style of the Daikokuya, however, was very much like those shown in woodblock prints of such other famous Edo-period shops as the Echigoya and the Shirokiya. This style probably reached maturity in the years between 1688 and 1735. Among extant plans of the time, there is one of a smaller shop that may well have been the forerunner of the Daikokuya main store.

The Izawa (in the present Mie Prefecture) residence of the Daikokuya's owner, built between 1684 and 1687, was in the richly gabled *yatsumune* style, which incorporated elements of temple and castle architecture and which persisted until the Meiji era (1868–1912), when it became possible to take photographs of representative examples. Fortunately, a plan of the house at Izawa survives to show what its interior comprised: an earth-floored passage along a shop area of eight-mat size; an eight-mat room with a Buddhist altar and latticed windows; an eight-mat office room; a board-floored kitchen-dining area of eight-mat size; a four-and-a-half-mat room with a sunken hearth; a small kitchen of two-mat size; three *zashiki* (rooms for sitting, sleeping, or entertaining guests) of eight, nine, and eleven mats respectively; a four-mat room for the master's personal attendant; and an earth-floored area of ten-mat size for the *kamado*, or clay-plastered cooking stoves.

The plan of the main section, which is eight bays by nine, is basically like those of houses in the

155. Minka *with* kabuto yane *(helmet roof), nineteenth century, Tamugimata, Asahi Village, Yamagata Prefecture.*

156. Misegura *(shop-storehouse), nineteenth century, Kawagoe, Saitama Prefecture.*

Kyoto-Osaka district. Attached to the main house in the back were a small four-room building and another small building that served as living quarters for retired members of the family. Today, however, none of the structures exist to show the scale on which the owner of the chain of dry-goods enterprises lived.

The Daikokuya's headquarters shop in Edo was fundamentally a commercial building, even though members of the staff slept on the second floor. In all cases of this kind the home of the owner was isolated from the shop and was less fireproof in structure than the thickly clay-plastered shop-storehouse itself. Valuables belonging to the family were stored in underground vaults, in built-in storehouses within the house itself (Fig. 10), or in independent storehouses constructed on the residential grounds.

Many of these residences had clay-plastered walls, but the clay, generally applied to the first-story front and back, was only ten centimeters thick. Clearly it was of less protective value in time of fire than the thirty centimeters of clay used on the walls of the shop-storehouse buildings. Fires of disastrous proportions occurred with alarming frequency in Edo, and it is scarcely surprising that during the Kyoho era (1716–36) many shop-storehouses in this sturdy fireproof style began to go up in the center of town. So much work did this building activity bring the plasterers that comment was made on it in a Kyogen comic interlude of a Noh-play program of the time to the effect that while the carpenters weren't unhappy at all, the plasterers were really riding a wave of prosperity. Moreover, although usually only the master carpenter's name was included in the paper decoration nailed to the ridge of an ordinary house when the framework was completed, in the case of these clay-plastered *misegura* (shop-storehouses) the plasterer's name also appeared. It is worth noting here that a considerable number of *misegura* from the late Edo period and the Meiji era remain in the city of

157. Kudo-*style* minka, *eighteenth century, Kishima County, Saga Prefecture.*

158. Clay-plastered storehouse with first-floor sitting room, nineteenth century, Aizu Bange, Fukushima Prefecture.

Kawagoe (Saitama Prefecture) today (Figs. 88, 156), although not a single one is left standing in Tokyo.

The first-floor openings and the second-floor windows of the *misegura* were fitted with heavy wooden doors covered with copper sheeting and thick layers of clay. In case of fire, the plasterer responsible for the building would close these openings and seal the cracks around them with clay kept handy for the purpose. So that the responsible plasterer would be immediately identifiable, each used a special mark.

I have already mentioned interior storehouses, but I might also note in passing that these too were built with thick clay walls, and, in spite of the fact that they had few windows, the finest *zashiki* in the building was always located on the first floor of the storehouse (Fig. 158).

In seventeenth-century Kyoto wealthy townsmen symbolized their affluence by erecting three-story clay-plastered storehouses, as the famous Edo-

period novelist Ihara Saikaku records. At one time these storehouses, which were generally three by either three or four bays in area, towered above the low houses of the city, but none of them are left today.

FARMHOUSES OF THE EDO PERIOD   In bringing this book to a close, I should like to call the reader's attention to some of the most common styles employed for *minka* in the farmhouse category. Although the term "style" often implies exterior appearance only, it seems more enlightening to consider structure and floor plan together with exterior appearance, since the former are clearly reflected in the latter, especially in the roof form. Most of the styles I shall mention here first began to assume shape in the Kamakura and Muromachi periods but did not reach maturity until the early Edo period. Of course, certain time gaps and lapses occurred in the process of achieving this maturity.

159. *Front view of clay-plastered Kumagaya house, eighteenth century, Hagi, Yamaguchi Prefecture.*

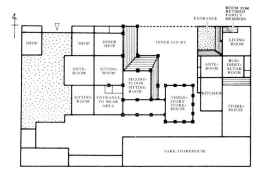

160. *Plan showing first and second floors of Tsuboyoshi, a combination shop and living quarters, seventeenth century (built in 1658; remodeled in 1697), Kashihara, Nara Prefecture.*

Magariya. The literal meaning of this term is "bent house" or "turning house." It is an L-shaped structure found only in a certain part of Iwate Prefecture, and the short limb of the L is a stable for horses. The people of this region of Japan began to capture and train wild horses when the Kamakura shogunate government, after sending land stewards to this part of the country, introduced the style of farming then followed in the Kanto plain (the area of which Tokyo is the center). When the house style took firm root is not entirely clear, but the word *magariya* appears in records of a fire that occurred during the Kambun era (1661–73), and it is therefore safe to assume that the style was well known by that time. The chief reason for including the stable in the main house was that of convenience in caring for the animals, but a certain unsanitary aspect is undeniable. The L-shaped plan probably derived from building-area restrictions related to width of frontage and ease of control of the whole structure from the living quarters.

Chumon. This style (Figs. 72, 118, 119), though similar to the one just discussed, differs from it in that the short limb of the L in this case comprises the entrance and the toilet as well as the stable. The entrance to the *magariya* is in the main wing. *Chumon*-style houses are found in Niigata, Yamagata, and Akita prefectures, where the severe winters and heavy snows explain the evolution of the style, just as the need for a convenient stabling place for horses explains that of the *magariya*. To prevent too heavy an accumulation of snow on the roof, the building must be tall, and its upper structure must be steeply pitched. Adding the short limb of the L—the so-called *chumon*—to the basic house helps stabilize the high structure. In addition, since the *chumon* contains the entrance, it serves the secondary function of a protective porch. Finally, it should be noted that going to an outdoor toilet is a hardship when snows are banked deep around the house. The *chumon*-style house therefore brings the toilet indoors but places it in a position where it can exert the least distasteful influence on family life. Variations of the style include T-shaped and U-shaped plans.

Kabuto. The word *kabuto* means "helmet," and the style takes its name from the helmet-shaped roof it employs (Figs. 106, 155). This is a variation of the hipped roof, which has been prevalent in the Kanto region since the Nara period. When the lofts of hipped-roof houses came to be used for breeding silkworms, both light and ventilation became essential. One of the methods devised to meet these needs was the *kabuto* style, in which parts of the ends of the roof were cut away to leave a trapezoidal area that was then fitted with board walls and openings for ventilation and illumination of the upper rooms. Since the resulting gablelike form resembles a type of helmet worn by feudal-period samurai, the style was given this name. The version of the *kabuto* just described is most often found in the Kanto district. In Gumma Prefecture, a single opening is made in the side of the roof parallel to the ridge.

Hommune. The literal meaning of *hommune* is "true ridge" or "main ridge." This style must have been in use by 1696, for the Matsushita house, built in Nagano Prefecture in that year, is a *hommune* building. The plan is nearly square, the roof is gabled and board-covered, and the entrance is in the gable end. There are usually an odd number of openings. The eaves, beams, and braces on the gable side produce a dramatically impressive composition, and the gable is topped with a soaring birdlike ornament called a *suzume odori*, or sparrow dance (Figs. 108, 121). Houses in this style are found in the Matsumoto district of Nagano Prefecture.

Gassho. These vast thatch-roofed houses (Figs. 11, 29, 69), whose sharp-pitched roofs have given rise to the name of the style because of an imagined resemblance to hands held together in a position of prayer (*gassho*), are frequent in Gifu Prefecture, especially in the village of Shirakawa, and in the Gokayama district of Toyama Prefecture. The *gassho* style is actually no more than an enlarged version of the *sasu* structural system discussed earlier in this book. The area enclosed by the *sasu* structure is usually divided into three levels and is devoted largely to the cultivation of silkworms. It is not a zone for living. In addition to silkworm culture, topography had an influence on the development of this style in that lack of flat land made it essential to build upward, for the region is one of steep mountains. Interesting variations in plan and roof form occur according to the location of the houses in question. Those in the upper reaches of the Sho River have entrances on the side parallel to the ridge, while those in the lower reaches of the river have gable-end entrances, and those about midway along its course may employ either of these two placements for their entrances.

Takahei. This style, which occurs in Nara and Osaka prefectures, is characterized by a gabled and thatched roof with a tile-topped main ridge. The gable-end struts are extended upward to form the center from which are developed low tile-roofed copinglike walls rising above the gable. The prototype of the *takahei* (literally "high wall") style may be found in sixteenth-century Kyoto town houses. The roofs of the copinglike walls rising above the gables employ the so-called Japanese-style truss (*wagoya*), whereas the rest of the roof uses the *sasu* system. Opposing rising diagonal members are fixed together at the ridge. Since this design is structurally unstable, the symbolizing of social status must have played a greater role than pure function in its development. The eaves of houses featuring this kind of roof are generally of tile and have a gentle pitch.

Shihobuta. Common on the island of Shikoku and around the shores of the Seto Inland Sea, the *shihobuta* (literally, "covers on four sides") design consists of a hipped and thatched roof with skirting tile-covered eaves all the way around it (Fig. 153). In the case of this style, size indicates the social standing of the householders, but the style itself remains unaltered regardless of how exalted or lowly the owner may be. In mountainous areas of the region where the *shihobuta* style prevails, houses without the skirting eaves are frequently found.

Kudo. This is a U-shaped style (Fig. 157). Actually the term *kudo* refers to only one of a number of roof styles common to Saga Prefecture and all characterized by beams that are always two *ken*

(3.64 meters) long, no matter what the floor plan may be. Rising diagonal members rest on these long beams and give shape to the roof, which in its oldest form is said to have had a main ridge that described a complete square. In some cases it is L-shaped and in others a straight line. When, as is most often the case, the roof is composed of several slanting planes and therefore has a number of V-shaped gulleys, special rain drains are required. These are constructed by lining up tiles, semicircular in cross section, on logs to form a trough that is led through the wall so that it may carry the rain water completely away from the house. The most complicated of these many-gabled roofs has seven projecting points, but it is seldom seen today.

No one has advanced a convincing reason for the design of such a complicated roof, although it has been suggested that it was favorable from a magical point of view. Some say that it breaks the force of typhoon winds and makes them easier to withstand; others claim that it evolved from nothing more than the restrictions imposed by beams of uniform length. This last explanation is related to the sumptuary controls imposed on most classes of Japanese society throughout the feudal period.

Finally, other scholars have suggested that this type or roof developed during the historical process of bringing together in one building the originally separate living and kitchen sections.

Futamune. Resulting from the construction side by side of two houses with single straight ridges, the *futamune* (two-ridge) style is found mostly in the plains of Kumamoto Prefecture. A trough of tile or wood in the valley formed by the two parallel roofs carries rain water away. The persistent use of two-*ken* beams in both roofs reminds one of the houses in Saga Prefecture (see above), and in some rare cases the two-ridge style is elaborated to the point where it resembles the *kudo* style. In this case, too, it is possible to imagine the gradual coming together of a number of isolated buildings of which most were constructed with beams of equal length.

Futatsuya. Like the *futamune* (and probably like the *kudo*) design, the *futatsuya* (two-house) design arose from combining two originally independent buildings, but in this case their positional relationships are not fixed, and covered corridors serve to connect them. The style is found chiefly in Kagoshima Prefecture.

The "weathermark" identifies this book as having been planned, designed, and produced at the Tokyo offices of John Weatherhill, Inc., 7-6-13 Roppongi, Minato-ku, Tokyo 106. Book design and typography by Meredith Weatherby and Ronald V. Bell. Layout of photographs by Ronald V. Bell. Composition by General Printing Co., Yokohama. Color plates engraved and printed by Nissha Printing Co., Kyoto. Gravure plates engraved and printed by Inshokan Printing Co., Tokyo. Monochrome letterpress platemaking and printing and text printing by Toyo Printing Co., Tokyo. Bound at the Makoto Binderies, Tokyo. Text is set in 10-pt. Monotype Baskerville with hand-set Optima for display.

TITLES IN THE SERIES

Although the individual books in the series are designed as self-contained units, so that readers may choose subjects according to their personal interests, the series itself constitutes a full survey of Japanese art and is therefore a reference work of great value. The titles are listed below in the same order, roughly chronological, as those of the original Japanese versions, with the addition of the index volume.

1. Major Themes in Japanese Art, by Itsuji Yoshikawa
2. The Beginnings of Japanese Art, by Namio Egami
3. Shinto Art: Ise and Izumo Shrines, by Yasutada Watanabe
4. Asuka Buddhist Art: Horyu-ji, by Seiichi Mizuno
5. Nara Buddhist Art: Todai-ji, by Takeshi Kobayashi
6. The Silk Road and the Shoso-in, by Ryoichi Hayashi
7. Temples of Nara and Their Art, by Minoru Ooka
8. Art in Japanese Esoteric Buddhism, by Takaaki Sawa
9. Heian Temples: Byodo-in and Chuson-ji, by Toshio Fukuyama
10. Painting in the Yamato Style, by Saburo Ienaga
11. Sculpture of the Kamakura Period, by Hisashi Mori
12. Japanese Ink Painting: Shubun to Sesshu, by Ichimatsu Tanaka
13. Feudal Architecture of Japan, by Kiyoshi Hirai
14. Momoyama Decorative Painting, by Tsugiyoshi Doi
15. Japanese Arts and the Tea Ceremony, by T. Hayashiya, M. Nakamura, and S. Hayashiya
16. Japanese Costume and Textile Arts, by Seiroku Noma
17. Momoyama Genre Painting, by Yuzo Yamane
18. Edo Painting: Sotatsu and Korin, by Hiroshi Mizuo
19. The Namban Art of Japan, by Yoshitomo Okamoto
20. Edo Architecture: Katsura and Nikko, by Naomi Okawa
21. Traditional Domestic Architecture of Japan, by Teiji Itoh
22. Traditional Woodblock Prints of Japan, by Seiichiro Takahashi
23. Japanese Painting in the Literati Style, by Yoshiho Yonezawa and Chu Yoshizawa
24. Modern Currents in Japanese Art, by Michiaki Kawakita
25. Japanese Art in World Perspective, by Toru Terada
26. Folk Arts and Crafts of Japan, by Kageo Muraoka and Kichiemon Okamura
27. The Art of Japanese Calligraphy, by Yujiro Nakata
28. The Garden Art of Japan, by Masao Hayakawa
29. The Art of Japanese Ceramics, by Tsugio Mikami
30. Japanese Art: A Cultural Appreciation, by Saburo Ienaga
31. An Index of Japanese Art